EVALUATING REFERENCE SERVICES

A PRACTICAL GUIDE

JO BELL WHITLATCH

American Library Association
Chicago and London   2000

While extensive effort has gone into ensuring the reliability of information appearing in this book, the publisher makes no warranty, express or implied, on the accuracy or reliability of the information, and does not assume and hereby disclaims any liability to any person for any loss or damage caused by errors or omissions in this publication.

Cover by Tessing Design

Text design by Dianne M. Rooney

Composition by the dotted i using QuarkXpress 4.0 for the Macintosh

Printed on 50-pound white offset, a pH-neutral stock, and bound in 10-point Bristol cover stock by McNaughton & Gunn

The paper used in this publication meets the minimum requirements of American National Standard for Information Sciences—Permanence of Paper for Printed Library Materials, ANSI Z39.48-1992. ∞

Library of Congress Cataloging-in-Publication Data
Whitlatch, Jo Bell.
    Evaluating reference services : a practical guide / Jo Bell Whitlatch.
        p.   cm.
    Includes bibliographical references (p.   ) and index.
    ISBN 0-8389-0787-3 (alk. paper)
    1. Reference services (Libraries)—Evaluation.   I. Title.
Z711.W45   2000
025.5′2—dc21   00-038052

Printed in the United States of America.

04   03   02   01   00   5   4   3   2   1

CONTENTS

PART IV
REFERENCE ASSESSMENT ANNOTATED BIBLIOGRAPHY
113

PREFACE

Several years ago, the American Library Association's Reference and Adult Services Division (now the Reference and User Services Association) provided a program at an ALA conference on gaps in reference research (Whitlatch 1992). The purpose of the program was to stimulate reference research and encourage practicing professionals to conduct research on reference effectiveness. After the program, many participants said, "Now I know the questions I am interested in addressing, but I still don't know how to get started doing the actual evaluation study." This practical guide is designed to get people started by not only providing information on the basic techniques that are commonly used to collect data for evaluating reference services, but also by providing examples of studies readers can use to get started. An excellent way to begin is to replicate, at least in part, other studies in the field. The selective annotated bibliography in this book is designed to provide a useful guide to study examples and will aid readers in getting started on their own evaluation study.

For the purpose of this book, reference services are defined as personal assistance given by library staff to users seeking information. This assistance includes answering questions at the reference desk, on the telephone, and via e-mail; performing quick literature searches; instructing people in the use of library reference indexes, reference books, and electronic sources; and providing advisory service to readers. The evaluation of library instruction in a classroom or laboratory setting and of online searching by appointment is not the focus of this book.

PREFACE

Part I of this work concerns planning and evaluation. Good planning ensures that the study's purpose, goals and objectives, design, analysis, and budget are integrated as part of the study process. Good planning reduces the number of unanticipated and often unpleasant surprises encountered during a project.

Part II discusses the strengths and weaknesses of the most common methods of evaluating reference services and provides some practical examples. Part III provides an overview of issues related to the collection and analysis of data, as well as practical advice on how to communicate the most important study findings.

Part IV is an annotated, highly selective bibliography of literature focused on the evaluation of reference services. Getting started in conducting a reference evaluation requires becoming informed about evaluation studies completed in other libraries. Surveying this literature can take considerable time. Because each annotation provides a concise summary of the purpose of the study and the methods used, the reader will be able to locate quickly those studies of greatest interest.

Work Cited

Whitlatch, J. B. 1992. Research topics from the program—unanswered questions: Gaps in research on reference effectiveness. *RQ* 31: 333–337.

1

Purpose
of the Evaluation

The most important questions you must ask are: "Why am I evaluating reference services?" and "What do I plan to do with the study results?" The purpose of your study should have the potential to improve reference service practice. In defining the purpose of your study, you must consider how you will judge the effectiveness of reference service: Are you interested primarily in how efficient the service is? Or are you more interested in assessing the quality and quantity of resources, such as materials and staffing? Perhaps your primary interest is not in either of these areas, but in evaluating the process of providing and delivering the service. Finally, your primary focus might be on reference service outcomes, such as the value of the service in the eyes of the user.

Assessing reference services requires adopting a set of performance standards. A performance standard is a description of the level of achievement expected of a person or organization. Performance standards provide yardsticks against which performance can be measured. As a first step in adopting performance standards, you should review your reasons for evaluating reference service in relation to how you will define reference service quality. There are many ways to define reference service quality, but there is no "right" way. Assessing reference service quality will require adopting a set of values because the performance standards used to define reference service quality will depend upon the particular values you adopt. Among the performance standards often used to measure effectiveness of service are (1) economic—e.g., cost effectiveness, productivity measures; (2) service process—e.g., measures of satisfaction with the service provided; (3) resources—e.g., measures of quantity and quality of materials, staffing, equipment, and facilities supporting the service; and (4) service outcomes or products—e.g., measures related to the quality of answers or information delivered. The following sections will discuss the values underlying each of these performance standards. Each section will include a list of typical reasons for evaluating reference service that are related to that particular set of performance standards. Examples of studies relying upon that performance standard will also be provided.

ECONOMICS OF REFERENCE SERVICE

Economic assessments of reference service concern the cost or productivity of reference service. If improving the efficiency of reference services, reducing reference service costs, or saving the time of the library user is a major reason for evaluating reference service, you might wish to study

1. The number of questions a reference librarian typically answers in an hour
2. The cost to the library for each reference question answered
3. The length of time users wait for service
4. The cost per use of reference information resources
5. The comparison of cost per use for a printed reference source and cost per use of a similar reference source in electronic format
6. The length of time users are willing to wait for reference service
7. The relationship between cost of reference service and quality of service product
8. The time reference service saves the library user
9. The time users are willing to devote to the reference service process

10. The value reference service adds to the information the user obtains
11. The value reference service provides the user in exchange for the additional effort expended
12. The cost per query of reference service delivered in person, by telephone, or via electronic systems

Studies relying upon economic assessments of reference services are summarized in part IV of this book, the "Reference Assessment Annotated Bibliography," under chapter 1, "Purpose of the Evaluation—Economics of Reference Service." You will find these studies to be valuable guides should you decide to focus primarily on economic measures of reference service evaluation.

QUALITY OF THE REFERENCE
SERVICE PROCESS

Assessments of the reference service process involve evaluating the various aspects of librarian and user interaction. Frequently this has been described in the literature as the "reference encounter." Library users often find the information they receive as a result of reference service difficult to evaluate. Some users do have the expertise to evaluate the information they receive and are using the service to save time. But for most users, if they knew the answer or had the expertise to find it themselves, they would not be asking for help. Therefore, they are often unable to adequately assess the accuracy, completeness, or currency of the information they receive. Users who lack the expertise to independently evaluate the quality of information tend to make judgments based on factors related to the process of receiving service. Was the service provided quickly? Did the librarian show an interest in the user's information need? Was the service delivered in a professional and courteous manner?

If user or librarian perceptions of the quality of the service process are an important concern, you should consider designing a study to evaluate the effectiveness of the service process. To improve the quality of the reference service process you might wish to study

1. User satisfaction with personal encounters at the library reference desk
2. Comparison of user satisfaction when the service is via e-mail or other electronic medium, over the telephone, and in person at the library reference desk
3. Librarian behavior toward the user, in terms of such factors as approachability, courtesy, and active listening
4. Librarian effort in answering the question, such as the number of sources consulted, and time spent with the user
5. Librarian knowledge, as measured by training, education, and experience, and its relation to user satisfaction with the service process
6. Librarian reference communication skills concerning interviewing and soliciting feedback from users
7. User communication skills in terms of describing the information they seek, and the situation for which they intend to use the information
8. User knowledge, as measured by training, education, and experience, and its relation to quality of the service process
9. Level of demand upon the service
10. The appropriateness and effectiveness of reference referrals to other information-providing personnel or agencies

Assessment of the reference service process is the set of performance standards which has been most frequently used in evaluating reference services. The service quality and customer service movements, with their strong emphasis on the service process, have stimulated additional research on reference services using concepts and methods borrowed from these fields. In part IV of this book, you will find many examples of assessments which focus on the reference service process. These studies cover a wide range of topics, including the process of selecting answer sources; quality service measures as applied to reference services; the impact of nonverbal communication; the user's willingness to return as a key measure of reference success; librarian behaviors; the interpersonal dynamics between librarian and user; and interviewing skills.

QUALITY OF REFERENCE
SERVICE RESOURCES

Assessments of the quality of reference resources are related to the physical or material resources that form an essential part of reference services. Reference resources include printed reference books and indexes, electronic reference sources, the adequacy of reference staffing, the types of reference staff, the physical arrangement of the reference desk, and the adequacy of the library or community computer network. The quality of resources is related not only to the amount of money allocated to reference services, but also to how effectively scarce resources are allocated among the many competing needs within the library and within reference services: for staffing, for printed and electronic collections, for physical building facilities, and for electronic equipment and network systems.

If improving the quality and allocation of the resources that support reference services is a major reason for evaluating those reference services, you might wish to study

1. The level of use of the reference printed and electronic collections, which should include both use by librarians assisting users and users consulting reference sources independently
2. The quality of access systems for major reference sources; for example, indexing and arrangement of topics in printed materials, and search interfaces for electronic reference sources
3. The adequacy of guides, bibliographic records, Web pages, and reference expert databases which provide instruction and assistance to users seeking to identify appropriate reference sources
4. The adequacy of hours of reference service staffing at the reference desk, for telephone service, and for answering electronic queries
5. The time required to answer a question using similar printed and electronic (e.g., CD-ROM or Web-based) sources, and a comparison of the quality of information provided by each different format

6. The effectiveness of various reference staffing arrangements; for example, a team of librarians, library assistants, and student assistants providing reference desk services versus a desk staffed by library and graduate assistants with reference librarians accessible by appointment

You will find many studies relying upon assessments of reference resources included in part IV of this book. You will find these studies helpful in designing and implementing your own study on any of various topics related to reference sources, including evaluating end-user searching; use studies of reference collections; the reference environment; reference expert systems; comparisons of the effectiveness of reference source formats; and staffing patterns for reference desks.

QUALITY OF REFERENCE SERVICE PRODUCTS

Evaluating reference service products or outcomes involves assessing the quality of the actual answer or information the user obtained as a result of the service. This set of standards emphasizes the benefit or value of the service to the user. Although the user often cannot fully judge the quality of the product received, user assessments play an important role in evaluating service products because the user is the ultimate consumer of the information product.

If improving the quality of service outcomes provided to users is a major reason for evaluating reference effectiveness, you might wish to study

1. The accuracy (correctness and completeness) of answers users receive
2. The degree to which users are satisfied with the information provided
3. The extent to which users report getting the information they needed
4. How helpful or useful the user found the information in resolving a problem, i.e., how the service benefited the user
5. The degree to which librarians judge the question to be completely answered

Many studies of reference quality have focused on reference service outcomes. You will find several studies in part IV of this book that will be helpful in designing and conducting your own study. One series of measures relies upon unobtrusive testing and has been used most extensively to evaluate the accuracy of answers. Other studies rely primarily upon user judgments of success or upon librarian judgments of success. Another set of measures relies upon observational data collected by librarians but analyzed by experts not directly involved in the reference transactions. Still other measures rely upon user judgments of outcomes, but also collect librarian judgments of outcomes from the same reference transaction.

SUMMARY

The evaluation of reference services has many aspects. The study you design will be determined by the performance standard you select and the values associated with that standard. When you design your study, begin by defining the purpose of your evaluation and the ways in which you hope to be able to improve reference practices. Do you want to focus on the efficiency of reference services, the support and quality of resources available for reference services, the effectiveness of interactions between librarian and user, or the benefit of the information provided to the user? Your focus should play an important role in determining which performance standards and measures you select. Your study findings and practical applications for improving reference practice will be greatly influenced by how you define reference service quality—by economic, process, resource, or service-outcome standards.

2

Evaluation Goals and Objectives

Once the purpose of the evaluation has been clearly established, study goals and objectives should be written. Goals should be relatively few in number and be general statements describing the nature of the evaluation. Objectives should be relatively narrow, specific statements that are expressed clearly and explicitly. Objectives should be written so that measures can be devised to determine the level of performance achieved relative to each objective. Objectives will define your standard of excellence—the minimum level of appropriate service for your particular clientele.

The purpose and study goals should determine the types of methods and measures you use to conduct the evaluation. There are many good methods of evaluating reference services, but each method has both strengths and weaknesses, which will be discussed in later chapters of this book. Because no method is without weaknesses, defining the purpose and focus of the study is essential before deciding the type of measures to use in evaluating reference services.

Chapter 1 discussed selecting the values that drive any measures you might use to determine reference effectiveness. This chapter will look at typical goals and objectives that might be developed within each of the following definitions of reference service quality: economic, service process, service resources, and service outcomes.

ECONOMIC ASSESSMENTS

Sample Goal 1

To provide the staff necessary to respond quickly to user requests for reference assistance.

Possible Objectives for Goal 1

1.1 Provide sufficient staffing so that no user waits more than two minutes before receiving assistance.
1.2 Train reference staff to limit initial service assistance to no more than five minutes when other users are waiting for assistance.

Sample Goal 2

To enhance reference desk efficiency and productivity.

Possible Objectives for Goal 2

2.1 Offer directional assistance at an average cost of one dollar per question or less.
2.2 Offer basic information assistance at an average cost of two dollars per question or less.
2.3 Offer in-depth reference assistance at an average cost of five dollars per question or less.

ASSESSMENTS OF THE SERVICE PROCESS

Sample Goal 1

To provide reference assistance that satisfies users seeking assistance.

Possible Objectives for Goal 1

1.1 Provide assistance that satisfies 90 percent of all users.
1.2 Provide assistance that results in 95 percent of users reporting that the reference librarian showed an interest in assisting them.
1.3 Provide assistance that results in 95 percent of users feeling that the librarian spent adequate time assisting them.
1.4 Provide assistance that results in 90 percent of users believing the librarian consulted an adequate number of sources.

1.5 Provide courteous service and positive nonverbal communication to 90 percent of users.

Sample Goal 2

To provide reference assistance that makes appropriate use of referral.

Possible Objectives for Goal 2

2.1 Ninety percent of users report that when librarians referred them, they were able to access and utilize the services of the information-providing agency or person.
2.2 Ninety-five percent of users report that the referral to another source was relevant to their query.

Sample Goal 3

To make effective use of feedback in reference services.

Possible Objectives for Goal 3

3.1 Librarians ask 95 percent of users for feedback concerning their need for additional assistance.
3.2 Librarians ask 80 percent of all users if they found what they wanted.

ASSESSMENTS OF THE
QUALITY OF RESOURCES

Sample Goal 1

To acquire reference resources that provide adequate support for answering queries received at the reference desk.

Possible Objectives for Goal 1

1.1 Ninety percent of user queries requiring dictionary and encyclopedia types of sources can be answered by the existing reference collection of encyclopedias and dictionaries.
1.2 Ninety-five percent of users report that they found relevant information concerning their query in the reference collection.

Sample Goal 2

To provide access to electronic reference systems that give results conveniently in response to user-initiated queries.

Possible Objectives for Goal 2

2.1 Ninety-five percent of all users receive results in response to requests within 2 minutes.

2.2 Eighty percent of users are able to perform a basic search that retrieves information relevant to their topic by utilizing guides and help materials provided by the reference staff.

Sample Goal 3

To provide high-quality answers to users' reference questions by means of the Web.

Possible Objectives for Goal 3

3.1 Provide accurate and complete answers for 80 percent of all student queries through the Web.

3.2 Provide subject guides that have relevant information for 50 percent of all user queries through the Web.

ASSESSMENTS OF SERVICE OUTCOMES

Sample Goal 1

To provide reference assistance that satisfies the needs of users seeking information.

Possible Objectives for Goal 1

1.1 Provide all information wanted for 90 percent of user inquiries.

1.2 Provide information that 85 percent of users judge relevant to their query.

1.3 Provide information that 70 percent of users judge to be important or very important in relation to their topic.

Sample Goal 2

To provide high-quality answers to users.

Possible Objectives for Goal 2

2.1 Provide correct and complete information for 80 percent of all factual inquiries.

2.2 Provide instruction in use of electronic sources that 90 percent of users rate as essential in locating the information they sought.

SUMMARY

Planning a good evaluation of reference services requires developing broad goals and specific objectives in the early stages of the study. Objectives must be clearly stated and quite specific. The development of detailed statements on the level of achievement expected permits the level of performance to be assessed accurately and realistically.

Characteristics
of Good Measures

Good reference measures must be valid, reliable, practical, and useful (Van House, Weil, and McClure 1990). This chapter will define each of these terms and provide examples from reference assessment studies of valid, reliable, practical, and useful measures.

VALID MEASURES

Valid measures accurately reflect the concept being studied. In developing valid measures for survey research, you should ask

1. Does the measure reflect common agreements and images associated with the concept you are attempting to measure?
2. Do the questions measure what you intended to measure?
3. Does the set of questions you have developed include all aspects of the concept you intended to measure?

Suppose you are designing a study to determine how frequently reference librarians provide accurate answers to questions. One of the questions you have thought about asking is whether users are satisfied with the answer received. If you do ask this question, you will not obtain information which tells you about the accuracy and completeness of the answer. In reality, users may be completely satisfied because the librarian was courteous and made a substantial effort.

The satisfaction measure often tells you that users were pleased with the service process, but does not measure the accuracy of the answer provided.

Even if you asked the user directly whether the answer received was accurate, the user may not have the knowledge to answer adequately. One of the most valid measures for accuracy of answers is to use questions and measures developed for unobtrusive studies (Hernon and McClure 1987).

You may be planning a study to determine whether people found what they wanted. Again, asking users how satisfied they are with reference services would not be considered a valid measure of whether people actually got the information they needed. Users often are highly satisfied with the service even when they do not locate the information they wanted. For example, the librarian may have provided very courteous and attentive service. The librarian may also have provided good suggestions for resources in other information centers that the user considers very promising. Consequently, the user is highly satisfied.

By contrast, a good example of a valid question to measure whether the user found the information needed is the following question on the Reference Transaction Assessment Instrument (Murfin and Gugelchuk 1987):

Did you locate what you asked about at the reference desk?

    _____   yes, just what I wanted

    _____   yes, within limitations

    _____   yes, not what I asked for, but other information or materials that will be helpful

    _____   yes, but not really what I wanted

    _____   only partly

    _____   no

Validity is also a concern in studies for which you are collecting qualitative data, such as data from interviews and focus groups. In designing your research you should consider

1. The impact of the researcher upon the setting—for example, will observers change the way in which participants behave,

thus resulting in data that does not accurately represent real-world behavior?

2. The values of the researcher—does observer bias, previous beliefs and experience, result in interpretations of observational data that do not represent commonly held interpretations?

3. The values and possible bias of respondents who are providing accounts.

For interview and focus group accounts, an important procedure used to preserve validity is to compare data collected from different sources and by different methods. This procedure is called triangulation. An example of triangulation in reference studies is to collect descriptions of questions asked and answers provided from both participants in the reference encounter—this serves to compensate for the partial views of both user and librarian and to present a more complete picture of the actual reference encounter. Using an independent observer to record the reference encounter is another potential method of increasing validity. Still another important method is to ask the participants to review the recording of an interview for accuracy. When participants verify the recorded information, you can be more confident that the record truly represents the participants' view and interpretations of events.

RELIABLE MEASURES

Reliable measures are stable and dependable, and provide consistent results with each repeated use. Many survey instruments use several questions or items to measure one concept. A measure of reliability that tests for internal consistency, alpha, is used to decide whether the items or subparts of an instrument measure the same concept. The most commonly used measure of internal consistency is Cronbach's alpha (Cronbach 1951). Reliability is also a concern in qualitative research. For interview data, consistent and careful training of interviewers is an important precaution to ensure that all interviewers ask the questions in the same way.

Whenever you classify data into categories, you must test to determine whether different reviewers can assign data to the same categories consistently with each other. To conduct such a test, you could ask users who indicated that they needed help in the library, but did not seek assistance, why they did not seek help. You then classify their responses into categories. The consistency with which the individual user responses are assigned to the same category by different reviewers is an important measure of consistency. When assigning categories to data you have collected, it is important to arrange for two or three different individuals to independently assign the accounts to different categories and then compare the results to determine how consistently the different individuals placed the accounts in the same categories.

One of the most common methods used in collecting data on reference services is to classify information queries as directional or reference questions. Conducting studies in which librarians select these question types is not recommended, however, because of evidence that librarians' classifications of these query types are not reliable (Kesselman and Watstein 1987). A more reliable method of classification is to collect the actual questions and answers provided, and then have more than one expert judge classify the questions.

PRACTICAL MEASURES

Practical measures require that the data be relatively easy to collect. Piloting instruments and other methods of collecting data are essential in assessing how practical your reference measures are. Practical measures are not only easy and convenient for the library to implement, but are also easy and convenient for users to complete. Pilot testing to determine user reaction to survey instruments, the length of time required by the user, and ease of completion is essential.

Because of the workload pressure to provide reference service to users, evaluation of such services is often viewed as a luxury and, consequently, never becomes a priority, either for management or for the individual reference librarian. One way to minimize this difficulty is to collect information as part of the service process that later can be used for evaluation. Reference librarians can use forms as worksheets for the questions they answer, quickly recording the question asked, the answer provided, and the sources consulted. These forms can be used as the raw data from which to collect information on type of question, sources utilized, and librarian estimate of success (King 1982). Another practical measure that requires little effort is the Reference Transaction Assessment Instrument (RTAI), a survey designed by Marjorie Murfin, Gary Gugelchuk, and Charles Bunge (Murfin and Gugelchuk, 1987). They have already done the work of designing the survey, have tested the instrument for validity and reliability, and will provide analysis of the data for a minimal fee.

USEFUL MEASURES

Useful measures provide information that can be used to improve reference services. You should ask yourself if the data you intend to collect will be useful in planning and managing reference services. Normally, reference service assessments should be related to achieving one or more of the following broad goals:

1. monitoring the effectiveness of present reference service programs, including the reasons for success and failure;
2. evaluating the effectiveness of reference service innovations; and
3. assessing the effectiveness of reference service policies.

For each piece of information you propose to collect, look at the three broad goals and ask if the information can be used as part of the library decision-making process to improve services, to identify innovative ways of providing service, or to revise reference service policies or priorities.

If you are considering collecting information on library patrons' gender, and you do anticipate finding some differences in evaluation of services by gender, can the results actually be used to change services? Suppose you find out that more women than men ask reference questions. Will this information influence the way you provide reference services? Collecting and analyzing data are also time consuming. Generally, you will not be able to afford to collect all the data you wish and will be forced to ask a limited set of questions. Therefore, you should examine the potential value of each piece of information critically before deciding to invest the time and money collecting this information.

SUMMARY

Measures of reference services should be valid, reliable, practical, and useful. Valid measures are those that measure the concepts that the evaluator intends to measure. Reliable measures are consistent. Practical measures are convenient and easy for both the library and the user. Useful measures provide data that has the potential to improve reference service practice. All measures and methods of data collection should be checked for validity, reliability, practicality, and usefulness in designing an evaluation study of reference services.

Works Cited

Cronbach, L. J. 1951. Coefficient alpha and the internal structure of tests. *Psychometrika* 16: 297–334.

Hernon, P., and C. R. McClure. 1987. *Unobtrusive testing and library reference services*. Norwood, N.J.: Ablex.

Kesselman, M., and S. B. Watstein. 1987. The measurement of reference and information services. *Journal of Academic Librarianship* 13: 24–30.

King, G. 1982. Try it—you'll like it: A comprehensive management information system for reference services. *Reference Librarian,* no. 3: 71–78.

Murfin, M., and G. Gugelchuk. 1987. Development and testing of a Reference Transaction Assessment Instrument. *College & Research Libraries* 48: 314–338.

Van House, N. A., B. Weil, and C. R. McClure. 1990. *Measuring academic library performance: A practical approach*. Chicago: American Library Association.

4

Surveys
and Questionnaires

ERIC NOVOTNY

This chapter is intended for the novice researcher who wishes to conduct survey research. It provides an overview of the important methods, issues, and questions involved. The basics of survey planning, design, and administration are explained in an informal, accessible style. The emphasis is on practical tips for conducting sound and effective survey research. No knowledge is assumed, only interest.

The present work necessarily provides only a brief overview. In such a limited space, it is simply not possible to cover in detail all the issues relating to survey research. The social science literature is replete with research articles and entire books devoted to survey methods. I have attempted to present here the most useful insights and observations from many of these sources. Those desiring more comprehensive overviews presented in a similar style may wish to consult works by Suskie (1992), Fink and Kosecoff (1998), and Zweizig et al. (1996). In addition, the chapter 4 section of the "Reference Assessment Annotated Bibliography" in this book provides useful summaries of many reference assessment studies that use surveys.

WHAT IS A SURVEY, AND WHY
WOULD I WANT TO CONDUCT ONE?

A survey is a method of collecting information directly from individuals. Such information can include subjective, or non-verifiable, data such as a person's thoughts, attitudes, beliefs, or concerns. Surveys can also be used to obtain objective, or verifiable, information, such as a person's age, income, or educational background. Typically surveys obtain this information by having the person respond to a set of questions.

While their basic objectives and methods are the same, surveys can take a number of different forms. Examples of survey research include a questionnaire distributed after a library instruction session; a user satisfaction form given to every person entering the library; a telephone survey of a random sample of city residents; and a small group interview with some students about the library's policies regarding lost book fines. Each of these methods will be discussed in greater detail later in this chapter.

There are many reasons for conducting survey research. The best way to discover what users want (or don't want) is by asking them. Surveys allow libraries to obtain a current measure of how satisfied patrons are with reference services, policies, collections, staff, and space. Surveys offer users a chance to offer their opinions on these issues. Librarians can learn what services might be improved, and what new services should be offered. In an age of increasingly tight budgets, survey results can provide a rationale for increased funding, as well as providing a basis for decisions when services need to be reduced.

Of course a survey is only one of the options available for obtaining information about people. Depending on the type of information you need, a survey may or may not be the most appropriate choice. Other methods include direct observations of patron behavior, or using existing records such as gate counts or reference statistics. Each of these methods has its own set of advantages and disadvantages, which need to be carefully considered before selecting.

Using existing statistical records is one popular way to ascertain information about reference services. Examples of the types of statistics typically gathered include gate counts of people entering the library, and tallies of such things as how many reference questions are asked or how many books are reshelved in the reference stacks. These numbers have their uses, but they often prove to be of limited value when policy makers confront hard decisions. Statistics typically focus only on the quantity and not the quality of our interactions with library users. They do not tell us how people might respond to new reference services, or how highly they value the services they use.

Direct observation is another popular method for finding out more about our users. We librarians informally observe our patrons every day. These observations form the basis of our perceptions regarding what our users want. When undertaken in a more formal way, observation can be a powerful research tool. When done properly, observation can provide a more naturalistic picture of user behavior. It allows us to see how patrons actually use reference services, not how they say they use it. This can be especially useful in areas where survey respondents might be expected to lie, such as when asked if they have ever brought food into the reference room.

If you plan to do formal observational research, you must be aware of your own potential biases. It is very easy to misinterpret another person's actions, especially if you are expecting that person's behavior to fit into a pattern. We all filter observed activities through the prism of our own experiences and expectations. These need to be acknowledged and accounted for at the beginning. Any assumptions about patron behaviors should be explicitly stated. One way to minimize this source of bias is to employ more than one observer, thereby decreasing the effect of any one person's individual bias on the reported results.

Of the three methods discussed, surveys are best used if the information desired is something only the individual can provide; for example, if you want to know people's attitudes about a change in reference desk hours. When conducting a survey, you should always be aware that the results report only people's perceptions and stated opinions, and may not predict their actual behavior. Results from surveys will usually be most effective when combined with data obtained from other sources.

Once you have decided to do a survey, clarifying the survey objectives should be foremost in your mind. No survey should be undertaken without a clear purpose that is explicitly stated. Deciding the objectives of your survey should be the first thing you do, as it will affect all the other decisions you make. Before you begin you need to answer critical questions regarding what decisions will be affected by the survey data, and how the data gathered will help in making those decisions. Ask yourself how the results will be used. How does the survey you are conducting add to existing sources of data? Will the new information gathered be useful, and will it contribute to effective planning? Are you prepared to make changes if the data reveals a desire for new or altered reference services? If the results of the survey will not affect matters one way or the other, then there is little sense putting in the time and effort to carry out the research.

GETTING STARTED

It is impossible to overemphasize the importance of planning in an effective survey. Many of the problems associated with poor results can be traced back to a lack of initial planning. It does little good after the survey is completed to suddenly realize you asked the wrong questions, or people answered in a way you had not intended. After the surveys are trickling in is not the time to discover that you have no one on staff who can perform the necessary data inputting. Proper planning and organization at the start of the process can eliminate many of these difficulties.

Conducting an effective survey will take considerable time and effort. Before beginning your project, everyone involved needs to be clear on the level of commitment in time and energy which will be required. A well conducted, thorough survey project can easily take a year to be completed. This includes everything from the initial meeting to draft survey objectives up to the submission of a final report. Of course not every survey will take this long, but many do. The task can be accomplished more quickly if everyone is able to devote themselves full time to the project or if outside help is hired, but in most real-world library situations this will not be the case. You will most likely be required to juggle the tasks required by the survey with your regular responsibilities.

To manage this process effectively, it is helpful at the very beginning of your project to create a checklist of tasks to be performed and goals to be accomplished. It should also be established early on which persons will be responsible for tackling specific tasks. A sample document is provided in figure 4.1 to assist you in your planning.

SELECTING A SURVEY METHOD: TYPES OF SURVEYS

Now that you've decided to do a survey, the question becomes which type of survey should you select? As mentioned earlier, there are numerous ways to conduct a survey: mailing questionnaires, conducting group interviews, calling people on the telephone, etc. Each of these methods has its own advantages and disadvantages.

Mailed Questionnaires
(Paper Surveys Mailed to Respondents)

Questionnaires are the most common, and therefore most familiar, form of survey research. This section discusses questionnaires distributed by mail and those administered in person. E-mail questionnaires have their own set of advantages and disadvantages and are discussed separately.

Advantages: The fixed format of written surveys provides consistency. Every respondent sees the same question, and receives the same set of instructions. Self-administered surveys encourage frank responses, and avoid any effects of interviewer bias. Respondents are able to complete the survey at their own pace and at a convenient time. This allows more time for thought and can encourage well-considered responses. This may be especially helpful if you are asking about complex issues, or about behaviors over a long period of time, where the respondent may need to take a moment to reflect. Survey questions can be designed to be easily tabulated, thereby enabling data gathered from a large number of people to be processed and analyzed relatively quickly.

Disadvantages: Mailed questionnaires provide little or no opportunity for direct contact between the respondent and the researcher. Ambiguous or poorly worded questions cannot be clarified. Surveys

FIGURE 4.1

Sample Planning Checklist for a Mailed Survey

DATE TO BE COMPLETED		PERSON(S) RESPONSIBLE
	Initial Stages	
_____	Identify survey objectives	_____
_____	Review what others have done on the topic	_____
_____	Obtain human subjects clearance	_____
_____	Choose a survey method (e.g., phone, in-person, e-mail, interview, or self-administered)	_____
	Designing the Survey	
_____	Investigate existing surveys	_____
_____	Seek expert advice (on-campus, via electronic discussion lists, from a professional association, etc.)	_____
_____	Write the questionnaire and cover letter	_____
_____	Pilot test the survey	_____
_____	Revise survey/cover letter as needed	_____
	Data Analysis	
_____	Determine data analysis needs, including special software requirements, if any	_____
_____	Develop process for inputting responses	_____
_____	Do a test run with small data set	_____
_____	Enter actual data from the survey	_____
_____	Perform data analysis	_____
	Mailing Procedures	
_____	Create random mailing list	_____
_____	Obtain envelopes and sufficient postage	_____
_____	Stuff envelopes for first mailing	_____
_____	Track returns, prepare second mailing	_____

Final Report

	Write report	_____
_____	Distribute report in-house	_____
_____	Distribute summary of results to general public	_____

Follow-up

_____	Conduct meetings with library staff	_____
_____	Review after 12 months to see what additional actions need to be undertaken	_____

rely on the accuracy of people's memory and recall, and questions about specific events or experiences, e.g., the patron's last reference interaction, may not always receive accurate responses. Written surveys also assume certain skills. You may not receive responses from those with poor reading and writing skills, or those with physical impairments. The respondents are self-selecting, that is, you only get back responses from those who have some interest in the issue. While this is usually regarded as a good thing, it may mean that those with extreme opinions are more likely to respond. This may produce results that are not indicative of the opinions of the general population.

In-Person Questionnaires

In-person questionnaires are those administered to respondents while the librarian or some other staff member is present. Probably the most common example of this type of survey is a user satisfaction form given to each person as they enter the library. Other examples are surveys given after a library instruction session, or to patrons who ask for assistance at the reference desk. In these situations you will typically want to confine your survey questions to those which are short and which can be easily answered. If what you are after involves a significant investment of time on the patrons' behalf, you are probably best advised to seek another survey method, or provide some sort of incentive for participation. The incentive need not be expensive or elaborate to work. Common items such as pens, buttons, or candy have proven effective at getting people to respond to surveys. Remember that your patrons came to the library for a reason, and it probably was not to complete a survey. Any efforts on your part to acknowledge this will go a long way in getting respondents to cooperate.

Advantages: Distributing a survey in person is usually cheaper than other types of surveys, due to savings on postage or telephone calls. Such surveys can also be conducted more quickly than mailed surveys, since there is no need for respondents to send something back. Typically the response rate is higher, and the presence of a staff member ensures that respondents can ask questions if they encounter difficulties while completing the questionnaire.

Disadvantages: Distributing a survey in person will not produce a good random sample. Most obviously, it will exclude people who did not use the library that day or at all. The presence of a staff member may make people feel compelled to respond, which can lead to distorted answers. If someone feels pressured to complete a survey, they may provide more negative responses than they would otherwise. This is especially true if the survey is long or complex. Conversely, respondents might overreport positive behaviors in an effort to impress or please the person collecting the information. The presence of a staff member also eliminates some of the confidentiality present in mailed questionnaires. Respondents may be less inclined to give truthful answers if they feel that their survey will be read by the person who is collecting the results. One way to alleviate this concern is to provide a closed box where respondents can return questionnaires. This preserves the privacy and confidentiality of responses.

Telephone Surveys

Telephone surveys are commonly used by librarians, social scientists, and businesses as a way to quickly reach broad segments of the population. Almost everyone has a telephone, and it is harder to ignore a telephone call than a mailed survey. There are issues to be aware of, however. Reaching some people by telephone can be difficult. Phone calls may also be seen as more intrusive than questionnaires on paper. Certainly anyone who has had a conversation or favorite television program interrupted by a telemarketer can appreciate the attitudes of some people towards unsolicited phone calls. The relative advantages and disadvantages of telephone surveys are discussed below.

Advantages: Telephone surveys will generally get faster responses, and need a shorter data collection period than mailed surveys. Conducting a survey by telephone *may* cost less than a mailed survey, depending on the costs of available personnel and local phone rates. This is usually true only if you can get volunteers to place calls. In most other cases, telephone surveys are more expensive than other methods. The response rate is similar to that of mailed questionnaires. A phone survey will reach people with minimal reading or writing skills, although it may exclude those who are not fluent in the language the phone survey is conducted in.

Disadvantages: Telephone surveys require that you provide training for all interviewers to ensure that they administer the survey properly. The phone offers little assurance of confidentiality and may not be appropriate if the questions are personal or sensitive. People may be reluctant to answer such questions honestly over the phone. A paper form is preferable if questions are especially long or complicated. A question that has a string of choices, or one where respondents are required to rank options, is probably best asked on paper. If you select the phone survey, you will not be able to utilize graphics or visual aids to explain concepts. Telephone surveys require persistence: some people may be hard to reach via the phone, or they may be busy when you call.

Focus Groups

Focus groups and interviews will be discussed in greater detail in the next chapter. For completeness a brief discussion is provided here. In a focus group, library staff collect information from small groups of people. This process is best used when complex issues are being investigated, and where context and feedback from interviewers is important. Typically the group's members are asked to respond to a set of questions. Observations and comments are recorded by staff members for further analysis.

Advantages: Doing a few focus groups may be easier than sampling a large population. Depending on how many groups are assembled, results can be obtained faster than with any other survey method. Focus groups allow respondents to express their own thoughts in their own words. You may discover problems or solutions you would not have uncovered using a less interactive model. A focus group is also more flexible than the other options discussed. It allows for free-form responses, and a genuine dialogue between librarians and the people whose opinion we are seeking. The give-and-take central to group discussions often proves effective in stimulating new ideas.

Disadvantages: Some respondents may be fearful for their privacy, or may not want to express controversial opinions in front of others. It may be difficult to convince others that the opinions of a small number of focus group members adequately represent the feelings of the larger population. Due to the freewheeling format of focus groups, the results obtained are difficult to quantify. Focus groups also require skilled group interviewers. A poorly prepared interviewer can seriously bias your results. In particular, staff members need to be wary of defending existing practices, and to appear receptive to negative as well as positive comments from group members.

Focus groups may be best used to identify the scope of problems, and to suggest areas for further research. They can be used to interpret the results obtained from a larger survey, or to help provide the "whys" behind quantitative findings For example, if a print survey reveals that certain groups use the library less often, a targeted focus group can help pinpoint the reasons why.

It should be clear from the preceding discussion that there is no one best way to conduct a survey. Which method is most appropriate depends on what factors are most important to you. If getting responses quickly from current library users is a primary concern, an in-person study may be the easiest way to obtain a large number of responses. On the other hand, if you have a long, complicated survey, you may want to opt for a mailed survey that respondents can complete at a time convenient to them. The quality of responses should always be a primary consideration. A few personal interviews may produce a number of high-quality responses more quickly and easily than conducting a mass mailing or placing hundreds of phone calls.

SAMPLING METHODS

In most survey research, it is not possible or desirable to ask every patron the questions you want answered. Sampling is a way to address this problem. A sample is a subset of a larger group. Good samples are the equivalent of their larger populations; that is, they share the same characteristics. For example, if the general population is 50 percent female, a good sample will have a comparable percentage of women in it.

In most cases, the best and easiest way to obtain a representative sample is to select respondents completely randomly. Random selection assures that everyone in your population has an equal chance of being surveyed. This makes it much more likely that your sample population will be similar to the overall population. If the survey sample is selected non-randomly, it can easily bias the results in ways that are hard to predict.

Typical ways of compiling random samples are by having a computer generate random numbers, calling every tenth page from a phone book, or choosing every twentieth name from a list of registered voters. You want to be very careful that the method you select is truly random. If you are using the phone book, there may be people not included such as recent arrivals or married women. Think carefully about your source for any random sample you select. If you have reason to believe that it may exclude some segment of the population, consider how this may affect your results. Be sure to note any possible sources of sample bias in your final report.

The other factor to consider in sampling is the size of the sample. In general, the larger the sample size the better. The larger the sample, the less chance there is for sampling error. Sampling error is the percentage by which you can expect your results to differ from the actual results if you had been able to survey everyone. It makes sense that the more people you survey, the closer your results will be to the actual population. A larger sample size reduces the likelihood of "fluke" results, where your results drastically differ from the actual population.

While larger is generally better, there is a point of diminishing returns. After about one thousand persons, each additional person added does not reduce the sample error significantly. Even large national polls rarely survey more than several thousand people, and for local surveys the number can be much smaller. For most purposes, a random sample size of 100 to 300 people is sufficient to ensure confidence in the results.

RESPONSE RATES

The term *response rate* refers to the number of people who return, or respond, to your survey. It is usually expressed as a percentage of the total number of surveys distributed. If 200 surveys are mailed and 100 are returned, the response rate is 50 percent. If you cannot handle rejection, then survey research may not be your favorite activity. Not everyone will eagerly return the survey you have spent so much time designing. In general, a response rate of 70 to 80 percent is considered good. This rate will vary depending on the survey method you select. Unsolicited mail surveys typically receive the lowest response rates, as low as 20 percent. In general you should strive to achieve a response rate of at least 50 percent. Of course, you need not throw away your survey results if the rate is less than this, but you will need to acknowledge that your data may not conform to the general population. Later on we will discuss steps you can take to increase the response rate to more acceptable levels.

The response rate is important because a substantial number of non-respondents can bias your survey results. Those who choose not to respond may differ in their characteristics or opinions from those who do choose to respond to the survey. The higher the response rate, the more confidence you can have that the answers received are shared by members of the overall population.

There are several steps you can take to maximize your response rate. Perhaps the most important is simply to be considerate. Recognize that for most respondents the survey is an inconvenience and take steps to minimize this. Keep the survey form short by asking only the questions you truly need to know about. Explain the relevance of seemingly unimportant questions and keep directions clear and simple. One effective way to increase responses is to show your appreciation by including a small gift such as a pin or a pencil.

All mailed surveys should contain a cover letter that explains the purposes of the survey briefly and clearly. The cover letter is your foot in the door, and its appearance and content are crucial. Take the time to draft a well-written letter that invites respondents to read further. Presenting a professional, "important" image will also help maximize response rates. Explain in your introduction how vital it is that your survey be completed. Respondents will react much more positively to a survey if they feel they are making a contribution to a worthwhile goal. Include in your introduction the project title and the sponsor's name, and be sure that the letter is printed on high-quality paper.

The aesthetics of the survey itself are critical to achieving a high response rate. The literature is replete with suggestions as to which color paper is most effective, how much white space is needed, etc. These can be summarized simply by stating that anything which can be done to make a survey look more professional is good. Professional surveys appear uncluttered, with plenty of white space and no grammatical errors. No matter how attractive a paper color you select, if the survey contains numerous typing errors the effect will be ruined.

Lastly, for mail surveys you will want to do a second mailing to those who have not responded to your initial request. Most people who will respond to a paper survey do so within the first week after they receive the survey. If after the first week your response rate is not at an acceptable level, a follow-up mailing should be undertaken. Usually this is done during the second week after the survey has been distributed. Your follow-up mailing should include a modified version of your cover letter indicating that you have yet to receive a response from them, and letting them know that you are still interested in their opinions. A second copy of the survey should be included, since many will have lost the copy sent in the initial mailing. Research indicates that a single follow-up mailing can substantially improve response rates. Additional follow-up mailings are not usually worthwhile, however, since the rate of improvement declines with each mailing. If people have not responded to your second request for participation, it is unlikely that they will be persuaded by a third appeal.

Surveys which are administered in person present their own set of challenges. There are a few steps you can take to ensure a high response rate in this type of situation. The most important of these is to employ friendly, flexible, polite, and persuasive people to distribute your survey. In most cases your patrons will not be overjoyed to participate in your survey. The person distributing the questionnaire will bear the brunt of this displeasure. How he or she approaches the respondent and establishes contact can make all the difference in the world.

Library staff who are administering a survey need to receive uniform training and instructions. Each staff member should be told the importance of the survey objectives so that this can be relayed to respondents. Those administering the survey need to be able to explain to patrons that their responses are valued. They should also have some idea as to how the survey results will be used to improve reference services.

When approaching people to complete your survey, the key words to remember are brevity and politeness. Survey administrators should briefly explain what they are doing and why the library needs the person's assistance. This is best accomplished by using concrete examples. Merely saying "this survey is important" will not impress many people. A better method is to provide a concrete example of how you intend to improve services based on the survey results. Another approach is to ask a question from the survey before giving the person the form to fill out. This technique is especially effective if the question is thought-provoking or catchy in some way. Once you get people's attention it is easier to convince them to take the time to complete the entire survey.

For telephone surveys, the main factor limiting response rate is the availability of respondents. You will want to consider how your calling patterns may affect your response rate, and, just as importantly, how this may bias the results you receive. The most obvious distorting effect occurs as a result of when the survey is conducted. If the majority of the calls in your survey are placed during the workday (9 A.M. to 5 P.M.), you are likely to reach a much different segment of the population than if the majority of your calls are placed in the evening or on weekends.

Persistence is the key to increasing response rates in telephone surveys. If you are unable to reach people, call back. Experience from survey research shows that you should plan on making six to ten phone calls per person to achieve an acceptable response rate from telephone surveys. This number is likely to climb even higher with the proliferation of voice mail, answering machines, and caller ID, which allow people to screen out unwanted calls. Calls made on evenings and weekends are most likely to reach people, so you should concentrate the majority of your efforts on those time periods. This requires a staff which can accommodate flexible hours. Staff conducting a telephone survey should be prepared to work odd hours during the data-gathering period.

As with the other survey formats discussed, it is necessary to impress upon the respondent the importance of the research being conducted. Your introduction should make this clear. A problem more unique to phone surveys is the wariness many people have toward giving information out over the phone. Due to certain telemarketing strategies and outright scams, many people are reluctant to respond to queries over the phone, especially if it pertains to personal information such as age, income, etc. Staff conducting phone surveys need to be aware of this, and be trained to effectively respond to this problem. They should take pains to allay any fears the respondent may have that the call is a ploy of some sort. This can be achieved in part by mentioning up front who the sponsoring agency is. Offer to provide a copy of the survey results if the respondent desires, and tell them that individual responses will be kept strictly confidential. Any additional information you can provide will help put the respondent at ease and help to convince them of your legitimacy.

PUBLISHED SURVEYS

Designing your own survey is hard work. As we will discuss in the next section, there are all sorts of seemingly innocent questions which prove complicated upon further review. One way to avoid this hassle is to simply use an existing survey. There are a number of surveys previously used by libraries, which are freely available. One particularly good source for identifying surveys is the *Reference Assessment Manual* (ERASC). A wide range of evaluation instruments are reviewed in this book, allowing the reader to select the most appropriate tool. Additional sources for obtaining sample surveys are Van House et al. (1987) and the SPEC Kits published by the Association of Research Libraries (1994).

In general, published surveys have the advantage of being "safer." They have been used before and presumably have had the "bugs" worked out of them. If you are using a survey of your own design, you run the risk of committing errors which may ruin all of your hard work. This is especially likely to be true if this is your first project. Published surveys also offer the advantage of cross-library comparisons. You can compare the results obtained at your institution with results obtained from others that have used the same survey instrument. This approach should be used with caution, however, since institutional settings may be quite different, making comparisons tricky at best.

If you choose to adopt a previously used survey, make every effort to contact the designers and get any advice they may have about adapting the survey to your specific needs. You can save a lot of time and effort by taking advantage of the experiences of others who have conducted projects similar to yours. A few notable surveys that have been widely utilized and tested include the RTAI, the resources provided by Nancy Van House et al. in *Output Measures for Public Libraries* (1987), and *Measuring Academic Library Performance* (Van House, Weil, and McClure 1990). For examples of surveys available on the Internet, see the appendix at the end of this chapter.

While previously utilized surveys save time, and may be the safer choice, the primary question to be asked is how relevant they are to your needs. Published surveys may not address the areas you are interested in. Avoid the temptation to adopt a survey simply because it has been published, or because a colleague has used it successfully. Be sure to examine each question in a published survey for potential bias or design flaws. Eliminate questions that are inappropriate or unnecessary for your library's needs. If possible, ask someone on campus or in the community with survey experience to review the survey for you.

DESIGNING YOUR OWN SURVEY

If you have opted to develop a homegrown survey, you will need to develop your own set of questions. Before asking the questions, you need to determine what type of information you are looking for. Generally questions fall into two categories, factual and subjective. Factual questions seek to uncover data about a person which are "true" and which at least theoretically could be verified through other sources. These data include age, gender, education level, marital status, etc.

When asking factual questions, you must take pains to be clear in defining terms. It is very easy for someone filling out a survey to have different assumptions than the ones made by the survey designers. For example, asking how many times someone has asked a reference question in the last week may seem like an unambiguous question, but the respondent may wonder if that means the last seven days or the current week. A better way to phrase the question is to be more explicit, asking how many times someone has asked a reference question in the last seven days. You would probably also want to define a reference question so that it is clear to the respondent what that phrase means. Are all questions reference questions, or only ones asked at the reference desk?

Subjective questions attempt to ascertain an individual's state of mind about a topic or an event. These may be trickier to ask than factual questions, especially if what you are asking about is not well defined or understood. One way to overcome this is by asking multiple questions. Instead of asking if the reference staff are friendly, ask respondents if they ever feel intimidated, nervous, or uncomfortable when approaching reference staff. By asking similar questions a number of times, you reduce any distorting effects that may occur as a result of the respondent misinterpreting any single question.

The standard question types in surveys include fixed choice, in which a respondent is given a choice between a set number of responses; and open-ended, in which respondents are given the opportunity to reply using their own words (see examples in figure 4.2). Fixed-choice questions are often used because they are easier to code and analyze. Limiting the number of responses available ensures that everyone is using the same terminology. Surveys made up mostly of fixed-choice questions are relatively simple to understand, administer, and fill out. The limited number of options may, however, force respondents to select misleading or inaccurate answers. Since it is usually not feasible to provide all possible responses, none may exactly correspond with the respondent's actual position.

FIGURE 4.2

Fixed-Choice Questions: Yes/No, Checklists, and Rating Scales

---

Did the librarian appear knowledgeable about your question?   ___ Yes   ___ Partly   ___ No

SOURCE: M. Murfin and G. Gugelchuk, "Reference Transaction Assessment Instrument," from "Development and Testing of a Reference Transaction Assessment Instrument," *College & Research Libraries* 48 (1987): 314–338.

What did you do in the library today? For each, circle the number that best reflects how successful you were.

	Did not do today	Successful? Not at all				Completely
Looked forbooks or periodicals	0	1	2	3	4	5
Studied	0	1	2	3	4	5
Reviewed current literature	0	1	2	3	4	5
Did a literature search (manual or computer)	0	1	2	3	4	5
Asked a reference question	0	1	2	3	4	5
Browsed	0	1	2	3	4	5
Returned books	0	1	2	3	4	5
Other (What?)_____	0	1	2	3	4	5

SOURCE: N. A. Van House, B. Weil, and C. R. McClure, "General Satisfaction Survey," from *Measuring Academic Library Performance: A Practical Approach* (Chicago: American Library Association: 1990).

How was the quality of service provided?

Outstanding :____:____:____:____:____:____:____: terrible

Comments on any special circumstances influencing quality of service: _____

SOURCE: J. B. Whitlatch, "Short Reference Survey for Library Users," from *The Role of the Academic Reference Librarian* (New York: Greenwood, 1990).

How often do you ask a librarian for help?

☐ Weekly   ☐ Monthly   ☐ Four times a year   ☐ Twice a year   ☐ Once a year

SOURCE: L. K. Wallace, "ALA Customer Satisfaction Survey," from "Customer Feedback—How to Get It," *College & Research Libraries News* 55 (1994): 64–65.

To assist people in becoming self-sufficient in the use of electronic library services, a variety of support may be required. What type of support would you need to be able to use electronic library services? (check all that apply)

☐ Detailed user handouts

☐ Technical information posted online, e.g., on the Campuswide Information System

☐ Basic instruction from the Library's reference desk service

☐ Detailed training and instruction in this area

☐ Computing and Network Service's help desk

☐ Access to computing equipment

☐ Other (please specify)

_____

_____

SOURCE: Association of Research Libraries, Systems and Procedures Exchange Center, "Your Library in Transition," from *User Surveys,* SPEC Kit 205 (Washington, D.C.: Association of Research Libraries, 1994).

Were you satisfied with the information   ☐ Yes   ☐ Partially   ☐ No
or materials found or suggested?

If *partially* or *not* satisfied, why? Mark all that apply

☐ Found nothing   ☐ Too much   ☐ Want different viewpoint

☐ Not enough   ☐ Need more in-depth   ☐ Couldn't find information in source

☐ Need more simple   ☐ Not relevant enough   ☐ Not sure if information given is correct

SOURCE: M. Murfin and G. Gugelchuk, "Reference Transaction Assessment Instrument," from "Development and Testing of a Reference Transaction Assessment Instrument," *College & Research Libraries* 48 (1987): 314–338.

How easy is it to find what you need?

☐ Extremely   ☐ Very   ☐ Somewhat   ☐ Not very   ☐ Not at all

SOURCE: L. K. Wallace, "ALA Customer Satisfaction Survey," from "Customer Feedback—How to Get It," *College & Research Libraries News* 55 (1994): 64–65.

It is important to avoid bias when composing lists of answers for fixed-choice questions. If you are asking about collections, you need to be sure to include print and nonprint ones equally, mixing traditional services with nontraditional ones. With the fixed-choice format, respondents will only have the options you provide, so extra care is required. Fixed-choice questions do have the advantage of reminding people of things they may have forgotten. If you just ask for the databases people have used, they may not remember them all. But if you provide a list of choices, you are more likely to get fuller, more accurate responses. This assumes, of course, that respondents are familiar enough with library terminology that they can provide an accurate record of the databases they have used.

Open-ended questions provide the opportunity for respondents to use their own words when discussing an issue (see examples in figure 4.3). This has the advantage of allowing for more complex responses in cases where context and meaning are important. For example, you might ask respondents to indicate what they like most (or least) about reference services. Respondents are then provided with sufficient space to indicate their opinions in their own words. Unfortunately, the open-ended nature of these types of questions means that the responses will be more varied and harder to analyze than if respondents were given a limited set of choices. The range of responses is literally endless, and all of these disparate comments must be organized before they can be analyzed. Some responses may also be unintelligible, or so brief as to be unhelpful. For example, what

FIGURE 4.3
Open-Ended Questions

What suggestions would you make to improve reference services?

What do you like most about the reference services currently provided?

How well does the reference collection support your needs?

Are there specific products or reference services the library should be offering but does not provide currently?

Are there any difficulties you have encountered while using reference resources or services?

is one to do when the response to the question, "what do you like least about the library?" is simply "the staff"?

Open-ended questions are best used when the issue being researched is complex and the potential answers are numerous. You should also consider using open-ended questions for topics that are controversial, where respondents may feel the need to express themselves more fully. A yes/no, fixed-choice format may fail to accurately reflect the depth of people's feelings on issues such as cutting reference desk hours, or reducing reference services. For topics such as these, it is important that survey respondents be given the opportunity to make themselves heard.

DESIGNING GOOD QUESTIONS

All good questions have one thing in common: they are easily understood by the people answering them. The questions you use should be unambiguously worded. If you are asking about an event, be sure to indicate the time frame involved. If you are asking for an opinion on an issue, define any terms used. Questions written in clear, plain language will produce the best results.

It is easy to generate confusion even if you are using common everyday terms in your questions. For example, if you are interested in how people's income level affects their use of the local public library, you might reasonably conclude that it would be a good idea to ask respondents to state their income. This question is not as straightforward as it might seem. Respondents will each have their own perspective on what qualifies as income. Does it include income from last year, last month, or just the last paycheck? Does it include the income of the entire household or just their personal earnings? Should only the salary be listed, or should the respondent include other sources of income such as investments? All of these variables can affect the figure provided. When designing a question, think about all the possible responses you might receive, and be sure to address these in your question so respondents know what information to provide. Using the example given above, if you do not want respondents to include investment income, be sure to indicate this in the question.

To reduce potential misinterpretations, it is recommended that every survey question have its own explicitly stated objective, including how it relates to the overall survey objectives. This need not be given to the respondents, but it should be central to the drafting of each question. The objective of the question will help you determine how best to phrase the question. Once you have your objective clearly stated, you can provide definitions of terms for yourself and for the respondent. Looking once more at the example in the preceding paragraph, knowing why you are interested in income will determine which types of income to ask about. If you do not define potentially ambiguous terms, respondents will be forced to guess which definition to apply.

BRIEF TIPS FOR
EFFECTIVE QUESTION DESIGN

- Explaining the question objectives will help people respond in the way intended. This is especially important if the question does not have an obvious rationale. For example, if you are conducting a survey on library literacy, you will want to explain the purposes behind any demographic questions, such as those involving age, sex, or race. Use phrases such as "This question is being asked to determine . . . ," or "Responding to this question will allow us to . . ."

- Use standard language. Avoid specialized words unless your objective is to see how many people are familiar with particular terms.

- Use neutral language. Avoid charged or biased terms. Even seemingly small changes in wording can affect results. When asked the following questions, a significantly higher number of respondents agreed with the first statement, although both statements express similar sentiments:

    Communists should not be allowed to distribute pamphlets in public.

    Communists should be forbidden from distributing pamphlets in public.

- Only ask for what you can get. Avoid questions of a personal or sensitive nature. If such questions are necessary, be sure to explain their purpose. Be aware of the social desirability phenomenon. Even in confidential surveys, people will select responses that place them in the best light. They will tend to overreport positive behaviors and attitudes and underreport negative ones.

- Only ask if you can deliver. Don't ask for opinions on a service you never intend to supply. If you cannot realistically expect to receive funds for increasing library hours, do not ask whether people would use the library if it were open more. Doing so can lead to raised expectations and to a lowered opinion of the library if it fails to respond.

- Only ask for what you need. It is common to ask for demographic information such as the sex of the respondent. Ask yourself if this information is useful to discover. What would you be willing to change if a gender difference in attitudes or opinions is uncovered? If the responses will not affect your actions, then it may not be worth asking the question.

- Questions should be close to the respondent's personal experiences. Make abstract questions more concrete by personalizing them. Do not ask if a reference service is useful: instead ask "do you use this service?"

- Avoid asking two questions at once. For example, do not ask if the reference staff is both helpful and friendly in the same question. It's possible to be one without being the other.

PILOT TESTING

Now that you've either designed your own survey or selected a previously used instrument, the next step should always be to conduct a pilot test. Think of this as a trial run for your survey, a chance for it to demonstrate that it is as good an instrument as you think it is. To do this you need to administer the survey to a small group similar to the larger one you eventually plan to poll. As much as possible, the conditions should be the same as when you actually conduct the survey. If you plan to do a mailed survey, then create a small group to whom you will mail the pilot survey. Your cover letter should be the same one you plan to use in the larger sample. If you are conducting phone interviews, then use the actual sampling techniques you plan to use later. Interviewers should be trained and completely ready to administer the survey.

You may think a pilot test is unnecessary for your needs. By this point, you or your committee have probably spent countless hours reviewing the questions and making adjustments, and you probably think that all the problems have been worked out. *Avoid making this assumption.* Test your survey out and see how it works under real conditions. This may seem like a waste of time, but it is actually time well spent. You will likely discover that a question you thought was straightforward is confusing to respondents. If you get unexpected responses, this may indicate a problem with a question's wording, or the set of options provided. Pilot tests can be used to uncover everything from problems with the instructions to mailing snafus. This stage is also a good time to examine your data-processing routines to ensure that they are set up efficiently and work as intended.

When conducting pilot tests, there are a few common problem areas you should keep an eye out for. These include respondents skipping questions, selecting more than one answer to the same question, making notes in the margins, or responding in ways that make no sense. All of these are indications that the test instrument is unclear in some way. If this occurs, you will need to examine the survey language to see where improvements can be made. Extraneous comments may indicate that you are omitting reasonable options from your list of answers. Skipped questions may indicate that the survey is too long or complex, or that the questions are deemed irrelevant. Questions of a personal nature may also be skipped. If you encounter respondents skipping questions in your pilot test, consider emphasizing the importance of the questions more, or including more information on their relevance. If your response rate is low, consider including incentives for participation. You might also examine your survey to see if it is too long or complicated.

E-MAIL AND ONLINE SURVEYS

Because they are relatively new, these types of surveys warrant separate discussion from the other, more established methods. The research literature available on e-mail and online surveys is still relatively sparse. A few recent works on the topic include Schuldt and Totten (1994) and Weible and Wallace (1998). While most of the procedures discussed for paper surveys also apply to online surveys, some additional considerations must be taken into account if you are considering conducting an online survey. As with any new medium, there are still questions about the advantages and disadvantages of survey research carried out online.

The research literature to date is consistent on the question of response rate. While rates varied, all of the studies conducted found a lower response rate for online surveys than for paper surveys. In a recent unpublished study, the Office of Admissions at the University of Texas at Austin sent the exact same survey to two randomly selected groups. Fifty percent of those who received the traditional paper and pencil survey responded. The response rate dropped to 20 percent in the group that received an e-mail notice directing them to an online survey form. These results have been replicated in the published literature on online surveys.

There are several factors usually cited as contributing to this lower response rate for online surveys. One theory proposed is that low response rates may be due to the inflexibility of most e-mail readers. They typically offer only limited font size and formatting options. Due to the variety of e-mail programs, most surveys will generally stick to the lowest common denominator. For online surveys this means opting for plain text. While using plain text may reduce the visual appeal of your survey, it does ensure that what you send out will look the same as what the respondent receives. If you use special fonts or graphics, what you send may be unintelligible to someone using an older or less elaborate e-mail program.

Convenience is also suggested as a reason why respondents prefer paper surveys to those conducted electronically. E-mail surveys often are not convenient for users, especially if the survey is time-consuming. A paper survey can be completed anywhere and at any time. An online survey can only be done while at the computer. For many users this may mean only at work, or while on campus. For this reason extra care should be taken to keep online surveys short.

Lastly, respondents to online surveys may have concerns about confidentiality, especially if the survey requires them to respond by e-mail. It is obviously difficult to ensure anonymity if the person's e-mail address is attached to the response. One way around this problem is to use e-mail to direct respondents to a secure Web site. The survey is then filled out on the Web and submitted using the browser's capabilities. This has the added advantage of making use of Web features to enhance the visual appeal of the survey. Surveys on the Web can employ additional colors, and offer push buttons and drop-menu options that are not available on many e-mail programs.

Interestingly, the University of Texas admissions office survey and other studies found no significant difference in the demographics of respondents. At least in the limited studies conducted so far, it appears that those who respond by e-mail are collectively the same as those who respond by more traditional means. This is somewhat surprising given the demographics of online users. Compared to the population as a whole, those with online access are more likely to be male, better educated, and have a higher income.

It should be noted that the studies conducted so far have focused on populations where e-mail use is common and accounts are often required. An electronic survey of the general population may produce different results. Despite the hype which makes Internet use appear ubiquitous, online access is still available to only a minority of the population. The 1998 *Statistical Abstract of the United States* reports that about 22 percent of the population used an online service in the last thirty days (Department of Commerce 1999). An online survey of the general population is likely to disproportionately exclude the poor, minorities, and women. If you are conducting an electronic survey, you may need to take steps to ensure that these groups are adequately represented. One way to achieve this is by doing a weighted sample, rather than using the random methods discussed earlier. In a weighted sample you deliberately include more people from the desired groups in your initial sample. This can help compensate for anticipated lower response rates.

Online surveys do have their advantages over other survey methods. Chief among these are time and money. Electronic surveys have the potential to be very cost effective, since there are no mailing or postage costs. These savings are only potential ones, though, especially if this is your first attempt at an electronic survey. There are significant start-up costs, including training and computer hardware and software. Unless you hire outside help, you will need to have a staff with a high degree of knowledge of several different programming languages and statistical packages. Once this is attained, however, each additional survey can be produced relatively cheaply. Once a survey is created online, it can be reused again and again with minimal costs involved.

Electronic surveys also offer the advantage of speed. Mailing time is virtually instantaneous. People seem to respond more quickly to e-mail surveys than to paper ones. Most responses are received within 24 to 36 hours, making the turnaround time very quick indeed. Results can be monitored continually, allowing for preliminary analysis only a few days after the survey has been distributed. Since the results are already in an electronic format, data entry is facilitated and data entry errors are eliminated.

As with the other survey methods, there are advantages and disadvantages to conducting survey research online. Whether this method is right for your library depends on many variables. Before conducting this type of survey, you will need to determine whether you have the necessary computer expertise on staff, or whether such expertise is easily attainable. You will also want to consider if you can reach everyone you wish to via e-mail or the Internet. While online research may very well be the wave of the future, you should remember that it is still in its infancy. Unlike other survey methods, it does not yet have a body of research literature and accepted practices. Results received from electronic surveys should probably be used with caution until the methodology of this type of research has matured.

ETHICAL CONSIDERATIONS

At a minimal level, an ethical survey is one conducted in an unbiased manner. Good faith efforts must be made to eliminate potentially biasing factors. If such factors are noted later in the process they must be addressed in the final report. Those reading the report need to have confidence that the project was undertaken in a professional and objective manner.

Of course, objectivity alone does not make for an ethical survey. All surveys involve real live human beings who deserve respect and privacy. If you are in an academic institution, it is likely that you will need to seek approval from the office responsible for research involving human subjects. Even if you are free of such formal constraints, you should take care to ensure that your survey is as unobtrusive as possible. Great care should be taken to avoid embarrassing, misleading, or otherwise emotionally harming respondents.

A few ethical guidelines should be applied to any survey research you undertake. First, all respondents should be informed and willing participants. They should receive an explanation of the process, procedures, and objectives of the research. No one should ever be pressured to participate. Coercing people to participate in your study is not only unethical, it is also bad research practice. Unwilling participants may give biased answers out of anger or just in their haste to be done with an unpleasant task.

All surveys should take extra care to ensure the privacy and anonymity of respondents. It should not be possible to link responses to specific individuals. If it is desirable to retain individual response sheets, assign a random number or use some other identifier besides the name of the respondent. Again not only is this ethical, but it is good methodology. You are much more likely to get honest responses if those completing the survey know that there is no way the responses can be traced back to them.

Fortunately, most library surveys are non-controversial and unlikely to cause emotional distress in respondents. In cases where you have doubts, you can seek guidance from a professional organization such as the American Library Association, the American Association on Public Opinion Research, or the Association of Research Libraries.

SUMMARY

It is my hope that after reading this chapter, and the others contained in this book, you will agree that conducting high-quality survey research is an attainable goal for any librarian who wishes to invest the time. Having read this chapter, you should be well on your way to successfully achieving your goal. You will embark upon your task already aware of many of the most common pitfalls and problems faced by survey researchers, and you will have learned strategies for avoiding such problems in your own research. While no work of such limited space could possibly address all the challenges you might face, I hope to have at least addressed the major ones, and to have given you a leg up as you begin your project. For those with questions beyond the scope of this work, a bibliography of additional resources on surveys and their techniques is provided in part IV of this book.

Works Cited

Association of Research Libraries. Systems and Procedures Exchange Center. 1994. *User surveys.* SPEC Kit 205. Washington, D.C.: ARL.

Department of Commerce. Bureau of the Census. 1999. *Statistical Abstract of the United States.* Washington, D.C., 573.

Evaluation of Reference and Adult Services Committee (ERASC). Reference and Adult Services Division. American Library Association. 1995. *Reference assessment manual.* Ann Arbor: Pierian Press.

Fink, A., and J. Kosecoff. 1998. *Survey kit.* Thousand Oaks, Calif.: Sage.

Murfin, M., and G. Gugelchuk. 1987. Development and testing of a Reference Transaction Assessment Instrument. *College & Research Libraries* 48: 314–338.

Schuldt, B., and J. Totten. 1994. Electronic mail vs. mail survey response rates. *Marketing Research* 6: 36–39.

Suskie, L. 1992. *Questionnaire survey research: What works.* 2nd ed. Tallahassee: American Association for Institutional Research.

Van House, N. A., M. J. Lynch, C. R. McClure, D. L. Zweizig, and E. J. Rodger. 1987. *Output measures for public libraries: A manual of standardized procedures.* 2nd ed. Chicago: American Library Association.

Van House, N. A., B. Weil., and C. R. McClure. 1990. *Measuring academic library performance: A practical approach.* Chicago: American Library Association.

Wallace, L. K. 1994. Customer feedback—how to get it. *College & Research Libraries News* 55: 64–65.

Weible, R., and J. Wallace. 1998. Cyber research: The impact of the Internet on data collection. *Marketing Research* 10 (3): 19–24+.

Whitlatch, J. B. 1990. *The role of the academic reference librarian.* New York: Greenwood.

Zweizig, D., D. W. Johnson, J. Robbins, and M. Besant. 1996. *The Tell it! Manual: The complete program for evaluating library performance.* Chicago: American Library Association.

APPENDIX

Survey Web Sites
(organizations, sample surveys, bibliographies, etc.)

Public Libraries

The surveys below are not specific to public-library reference services, but they may provide ideas for ways to organize and word your own survey.

http://www.vrtualfred.com/ccpl_survey/ccpl_survey.htm

> Feedback form for the Charles County Public Library, Md. The survey is hosted by a Maryland computer company as a public service.

http://npl.org/Pages/ContactUs/survey.html

> Online user survey for the Newark, N.J., Public Library.

http://ashlandma.com/library/survey.htm

> Example of an extensive online survey from the Ashland Public Library.

Academic Libraries

http://www.lib.uconn.edu/survey/

> Discussion of the survey results from a 1996 University of Connecticut faculty survey. In addition to the test instrument, the lengthy report details the survey methodology, results, and recommendations.

http://orpheus.ucsd.edu/survey/index.html

> Results from a survey performed by the University of California, San Diego. In addition to the report, three survey instruments are provided. Questions pertaining to reference are scattered throughout the survey instruments.

http://dizzy.library.arizona.edu/cust_survey/mail.html

> The University of Arizona's "Library Report Card," an ongoing online survey.

http://www.lib.duke.edu/staff/orgnztn/lubans/firstyear.html

Detailed report of a survey conducted by John Lubans on how students use the Web. Includes a copy of the survey instrument.

Other Internet Resources

http://www.inquisite.com

Web site for a company offering a survey tool which can be used to create electronic surveys in various formats.

http://www.arl.org/transform/us/index.html

Electronic issue of the publication *Transforming Libraries*. This issue is entitled "After the User Survey: What Then?" The page includes a very useful bibliography of printed resources, as well as links to libraries that are conducting online surveys.

http://www.aapor.org/

Home page for the American Association on Public Opinion Research. Includes the organization's code of ethics, and the table of contents to *Public Opinion Quarterly*.

http://www.arl.org/

Home page for the Association of Research Libraries. Includes a section with resources and links pertaining to performance measures.

5

Observation

This chapter discusses the value of observation as a method of evaluating reference services. The topics covered include when to use observation instead of other assessment methods; how to plan an observational study; the forms of observational methods and their use in assessing reference services; the design of observational studies; and ethical issues. This chapter provides a brief overview and is intended to supply you with enough information to determine whether observation will be useful in your own reference evaluation project.

WHAT IS AN OBSERVATIONAL STUDY, AND WHY WOULD I WANT TO CONDUCT ONE?

Observational studies collect information on processes as they occur in real-life situations. Observations may take many forms: direct observation, observers disguised as patrons, self-observation (e.g., diaries or daily journals), recording devices, physical traces, and examination of existing data collected for another reason.

Observation is a more reliable measure of how people actually behave, whereas questionnaires record how people intend to behave, or think they will behave, independent of a specific situation. Observation generally provides more in-depth information about situational contexts than do questionnaires or focus groups. By contrast, questionnaires and focus groups are more useful for measuring attitudes, opinions, and perceptions.

Observation is most valuable when the focus of the evaluation concerns what people actually do. Observation can also be used as an important check on the validity of a study that relies primarily on questionnaires or focus groups. People sometimes behave differently than they say they will! For example, your questionnaire results might indicate that 20 percent of all users say they will use reference desk services more frequently if they were available from 8 to 10 P.M. on Monday through Thursday. To test whether user intentions are an accurate reflection of their actual behavior, the library might revise its reference desk schedule, publicize the new 8 to 10 P.M. hours widely, and check to see how reference-desk usage patterns change by comparing two previous semesters with two semesters using the revised hours.

Observation methods are often more expensive than questionnaires or focus groups. One reason is that safeguarding against bias can increase the costs. Observer bias may color the type of data which are collected by an observer. Observational methods are more likely to provide biased results if only one observer is present. Bias can often be introduced if the "subjects" are aware that they are being studied. People will often behave somewhat differently when someone is observing their behavior (Weech and Goldhor 1982).

GETTING STARTED

If you decide that observational methods are essential to meeting your evaluation goals, careful planning of the study will improve the investment of time and the quality of your results. A sample planning checklist (figure 5.1) has been provided to assist you in this task. Effective planning must include discussion with other staff involved in the study, incorporation of their suggestions into the study when possible, and identification of adequate resources and budget to support the study, as well as procedures for each step. You should include an outline of the sequence of events, the person responsible for each phase, dates, and costs involved as part of the planning documents.

FIGURE 5.1
Sample Planning Checklist for an Observational Study

---

1. Select an observational method
   Procedures: _____ consult colleagues; _____ review literature
   Budget and Resources: _____ estimate time required

2. Determine sampling method
   Procedures: _____ consult with expert
   Budget and Resources: _____ fee for consultation?

3. Design observational forms
   Procedures: _____ review literature for similar studies
   Budget and Resources: _____ estimate time required

4. Address ethical concerns
   Procedures: _____ consult with human subjects review board
   Budget and Resources: _____ estimate time required

5. Plan data analysis method
   Procedures: _____ consult literature for similar studies; _____ consult with expert
   Budget and Resources: _____ estimate time required

6. Pilot test forms
   Procedures: _____ recruit participants
   Budget and Resources: _____ fees for participants; _____ copy expenses

7. Revise form based on pilot test results
   Procedures: _____ review results
   Budget and Resources: _____ estimate time required

8. Administer the collection of data
   Procedures: _____ obtain organizational consent; _____ obtain participant
   agreement
   Budget and Resources: _____ estimate time required; _____ fees for participants

9. Analyze data collected
   Procedures: _____ review data and organize
   Budget and Resources: _____ software program; _____ estimate time required

10. Communicate the results

    Procedures: _____ draft and revise report

    Budget and Resources: _____ copy expenses

SELECTING AN OBSERVATIONAL METHOD

A wide range of observational techniques has been used effectively in reference evaluation. To assist you in determining which might best meet your evaluation goals, each method is discussed and examples of studies are provided.

Direct Observation

When you use direct observation, librarians and users are aware that a study is being conducted and that their behavior is being observed and recorded in some manner. Direct observation of reference transactions has not been that common because of concerns about influencing user and librarian behavior. But studies involving direct observation of reference encounters do exist (Ingwersen 1982; Kazlauskas 1976; Lynch 1978).

Although there is some evidence that direct observation does bias the results by having an influence upon user success rates, it does not appear to be a large effect. Crews lists eight studies in which librarians were aware of being tested and notes that accuracy rates were only slightly higher in studies using direct observation than rates in studies using unobtrusive techniques where librarians were not aware that their performance was being observed (Crews 1988). Direct observation has the potential to change user behavior as well. People may not wish to be observed, for example, in the process of asking a question which they feel displays their ignorance.

Some of the concerns related to direct observation can be addressed by carefully and systematically structuring observations. This technique can reduce observer bias and can help focus on the types of information you wish to collect. Figure 5.2 provides an example of a structured observation form that can be used for collecting information on reference librarian behaviors. The Guidelines for Behav-

FIGURE 5.2

Model Reference Behaviors Checklist by Gers and Seward*

	YES	NO	EXAMPLES (Verbatim)
Approachability			
Smiles	_____	_____	_____
Makes Eye Contact	_____	_____	_____
Gives Friendly Verbal Greeting	_____	_____	_____
Is at Same Level as Patron	_____	_____	_____
Comfort			
Maintains Eye Contact	_____	_____	_____
Shows Relaxed Body Posture	_____	_____	_____
Makes Attentive Comments ("I see," "uh-huh")	_____	_____	_____
Speaks in Interested, Helpful Tone	_____	_____	_____
Interest			
Maintains Eye Contact	_____	_____	_____
Is Mobile, Goes with Patron	_____	_____	_____
Gives Patron Full Attention	_____	_____	_____
Negotiation			
Asks Open Questions	_____	_____	_____
Probes	_____	_____	_____
Paraphrases	_____	_____	_____
Clarifies	_____	_____	_____
Informs	_____	_____	_____
Checks Out	_____	_____	_____
Summarizes	_____	_____	_____
Uses Basic Questions	_____	_____	_____
Goes beyond Immediate Resources	_____	_____	_____
Cites the Source	_____	_____	_____

	YES	NO	EXAMPLES (Verbatim)
Follow-up (Evaluation)			
Asks "Does this completely answer your question?"	_____	_____	_____
Closes the Interview Tactfully	_____	_____	_____

*From L. S. Dyson, "Improving Reference Services: A Maryland Training Program Brings Positive Results," *Public Libraries* 31 (1992): 284–289.

ioral Performance of Reference and Information Services Professionals, available online at http://www.ala.org/rusa/stnd_behavior.html, provides a more extensive list of reference librarian behaviors that can be used to develop a behavioral checklist. Users have also been directly observed using online catalogs. Figure 5.3 presents an observation form for collecting data on user behavior at online catalogs.

Observers Disguised as Patrons

Unobtrusive testing has been the observation method most frequently used in evaluating reference services. Studies relying on unobtrusive testing typically use predetermined test questions that are put to reference librarians by proxies. Proxies are people who pose as library users and have received training in how to administer the test questions to unsuspecting reference librarians. The main goal of the classic unobtrusive studies, such as those developed by Crowley and Childers (1971) and Hernon and McClure (1987), has been to measure reference accuracy, that is, the degree to which reference librarians' answers are correct and complete. Many types of questions do not have precise answers, and thus the level of accuracy of answer is difficult or impossible to determine. Accuracy of answers will not be a useful measure of success when answers to queries consist primarily of advice on search strategies or instruction on using a particular database.

Unobtrusive studies take considerable time to design and administer. Test questions should be representative of typical questions received at the reference desk, especially in regard to the subjects of

FIGURE 5.3

Observation Instrument Used in Study of Patrons' Online Catalog Search Success*

_____

As Person Sits Down, Approach

Hello, my name is _____. I am a librarian here at San Jose
State University.

The Library staff is surveying people who use the online catalog to determine how they use it
and how satisfied they are with materials they locate through use of the online catalog..

Would you be willing to participate? I will observe your search, and ask you to complete a short
survey when you finish. It won't take long and will be very helpful to the Library in understanding how the online catalog is being used to help people find what they need. Your participation
is completely voluntary—if you decide not to participate you won't be deprived of any Library or
University services. We will make certain that none of the information we collect can be traced
back to any individual participants.

If yes, (you say) "here is a sheet that you can use as scratch paper (Form D—Did You Find It?)
to write down items you want to find in the book stacks later and then turn in by the box at the
exit" (point to box which says Return Survey Forms Here).

As Person Does Search   Librarian Form _____ B

(Do not offer help: However, if asked, note what you answered; Don't give person more than
necessary to answer the question; i.e., don't go on to tell people about other features you think
might be helpful).

Time Search Started: _____ (AM PM)
                    (Hours and Minutes)   (Circle One)

Use the Check Sheet to Note Observations

OBSERVATION

1. *Features Used in Online Catalog*

EASE OF USE (Check if feature used)

	Used (number in order used starting with 1)	No Problems	Some Difficulty	Considerable Difficulty
Author	_____	_____	_____	_____
Title	_____	_____	_____	_____
Keyword	_____	_____	_____	_____
Subject Heading	_____	_____	_____	_____
Call No.	_____	_____	_____	_____
Standard No.	_____	_____	_____	_____
OCLC No.	_____	_____	_____	_____
Reserve Lists	_____	_____	_____	_____

2. *Other Features Used (Check those that apply)*

_____ Display (Check those used)

    _____ title and author

    _____ title, locations, and call no.

    _____ locations and call no.

    _____ author

    _____ more of heading

    _____ subject headings only

_____ Limit search (Check those used)

    _____ words in the subject

    _____ words in the title

    _____ words in the author

    _____ year of publication

    _____ publisher

    _____ material type

    _____ language

    _____ where item is located

_____ Encountered the
Limit for Searching (Describe what they did)

_____

_____

    _____ (S) show items with the same subject

    _____ (Z) show items nearby on shelf

    _____ (W) same search as word search

    _____ Browse through lists

        _____ author   _____ subject

        _____ title   _____ call no.

(continued)

FIGURE 5.3 (continued)

3. *Did the user stop at the summary screen with only location and call number (rather than proceed to detailed screen listing circulation status)?*

_____ no   _____ yes

4. *Special Conditions (Check those that apply)*

_____ book not in collection (known item search)

_____ book in collection but in status other than "check shelves" (known item search)

_____ technical catalog/database problems

_____ difficult citation

Time Search Ended: _____ (AM PM)
                        (Hours and Minutes)   (Circle One)

_____

*Instrument is available through the Health and Psychosocial Instruments (HaPI) database. Behavioral Measurement Database Services, P.O. Box 110287, Pittsburgh, PA 15232-0787.

---

questions and their level of difficulty. Test questions should also represent the full range and types of questions that are asked. Collecting samples of actual questions asked by library users at a particular reference desk prior to conducting an unobtrusive study is an excellent way to identify representative questions.

Unobtrusive testing has also been used to evaluate librarian behavior and its relationship to reference success. A form created by Joan Durrance provides an excellent model for those who wish to use this method to assess the effectiveness of librarian behavior. Figure 5.4 contains sample questions from Durrance's "Reference Interview Checklist." The complete form is available in the *Reference Assessment Manual* (ERASC).

Self-Observation

Usually, self-observation takes the form of a diary or journal of regular activities. Diaries or journals are an important method of collecting reliable information from respondents because their recall of past

FIGURE 5.4
Sample Questions from Reference Interview Checklist*

1. Check one of the following statements which BEST describes what you saw as you approached the library staff member for help.
The staff member was:

_____ free to assist you

_____ assisting other patron(s) at the reference desk

_____ away from the reference desk

_____ on telephone or talking with staff member

_____ doing other work at reference desk
(specify type of work, if noted) _____

2. If the staff member was engaged in an activity when approached (see question no. 1), did (s)he acknowledge your presence?

_____ yes _____ no _____ not applicable

3. State the question you initially asked:

4. State the initial response—*repeat the first actual words used by the staff member to respond to your request.*

10. The style, interviewing skill, and strategy used by the staff member each contribute to the relative success or failure of the reference interview. Based on your interaction, please evaluate the specific characteristics below.

CHARACTERISTIC OR BEHAVIOR	LEVEL OF PERFORMANCE				
	Not at all			Very much	
To what extent did (s)he:					
show (s)he was approachable	1	2	3	4	5
appear to be interested in your question	1	2	3	4	5
respond courteously	1	2	3	4	5
appear to be non-judgmental	1	2	3	4	5
show confidence	1	2	3	4	5
make you feel comfortable throughout the interaction	1	2	3	4	5

(continued)

FIGURE 5.4 (continued)

12. At the end of the interaction, did the staff member use a follow-up question, i.e., some kind of question to let you know that (s)he was interested in finding out whether you got what you needed?

_____ yes _____ no

Explain: What did she say or do?

14. Given the nature of this interaction, if you had the option, WOULD YOU RETURN to this staff member with another question?

_____ yes _____ no _____ not sure

---

*From J. Durrance, "Reference Interview Checklist," *Reference Assessment Manual*, Evaluation of Reference and Adult Services Committee (ERASC), Reference and Adult Services Division, American Library Association (Ann Arbor: Pierian, 1995).

---

events may not be all that accurate. For example, if you ask "How many times have you asked for help at the reference desk in the past semester?" the information you receive will only be someone's best estimate based upon their recall of events over a three-month period.

When used to collect information on reference activities, self-observation studies usually involve librarians or users keeping logs of their various activities during the day and how much time they spend on each of those activities. Sample logs of activities conducted at the reference desk can be quite useful in determining how reference librarians actually use their time. However, reference desk work is fast paced. Diary or journal activities may seriously interfere with service to users, so librarians are not very enthusiastic about keeping any logs of activities while they are on the desk. Geraldine King has designed a form (figure 5.5) that requires a minimum of additional work (1982). This form is most useful for collecting data that can be analyzed and categorized by reference experts who are not immediately involved in the reference transaction. As more reference work is done off the desk through appointment, via e-mail, and in other settings where recording is less inconvenient than it is in the

FIGURE 5.5
Reference Transaction Slip*

_____ not started   _____ call with info   _____ check OCLC
_____ call to clarify   _____ patron will call

☐   Date _____ Time _____ Telephone _____

Author/Title _____

_____

Question _____

_____

_____

_____

_____

_____

Name _____   Tel. No. _____

Address _____   Bar Code _____

Sources Checked: _____

_____ Out   _____

_____ Request   _____

_____ NIL   _____

_____ ILL   _____

_____ Referral to _____

Total
Count   ☐

Initials (LIBN.) _____

---

*From G. King, "Reference Transaction Slip," _Reference Assessment Manual,_ Evaluation of Reference and Adult Services Committee (ERASC), Reference and Adult Services Division, American Library Association (Ann Arbor: Pierian, 1995).

typical reference-desk situation, self-observation may be used more frequently.

Users have also been asked to keep records of their information-seeking activities (Kuhlthau 1988a, 1988b, 1988c). The diary method is most effective if followed by interviews with the respondents, asking them detailed questions about the nature of their diary entries. If a diary is to be used as part of the study, forms should be prepared that can be used for the journal entries. A checklist of materials for diaries is provided in figure 5.6. Structured or focused diaries are recommended over unstructured diaries because of the expense of analyzing and recording a large mass of information.

Recording Devices

Actual reference encounters can also be recorded. The permission of both librarian and users must be sought prior to recording the data. Moreover, analyzing the extensive descriptive data can be difficult because it must be summarized, put into categories, and interpreted. This method is intrusive and time-consuming and is thus used less frequently for reference assessment. Studies by Lynch (1978) and Von Seggern (1989) provide detailed information that is useful for conducting observational studies using recording devices.

FIGURE 5.6
Checklist of Materials Recommended for Diary Entries

1. Instructions on how to complete the diary, including importance of recording at the time of the event

2. An example of a diary entry

3. Checklists of items to be included in the diary

4. Typical lists of activities

5. Open space at the end for observations, comments, experience with the process, and notes on how typical the respondent's activities were during this time period

Physical Traces

Papers can be placed in reference books to determine if those books have been used. Arrigona and Mathews (1988) used table counts (of unshelved materials) as an indirect method to measure patron use, combined with tally sheets that recorded reference librarians' use of materials. Although tally sheets and spine marking are two common techniques used in reshelving studies, automation provides an additional tool by recording the item numbers on the bar codes of all reshelved items (Welch, Cauble, and Little 1997). Data collected through these methods can be used to manage reference collections, such as purchasing, bindery, and weeding decisions, and to plan reference budgets and services to users.

Existing Data

Existing data can also be used to assess reference services. Transaction log records from online catalogs and other electronic databases can be kept to determine not only how frequently the databases have been used, but also the pattern of usage, patron failure rates, and the causes of failure (Peters 1989). A study by Hunter (1991) provides a good example of a transaction log study that assists reference librarians in understanding how patrons use the online catalog. Alone, these data are somewhat limited in their usefulness for reference evaluation. But when combined with other data collection methods, transaction log analysis can greatly enrich an evaluation study. For example, transaction log studies can be used in combination with survey data about attitudes: the transaction logs provide objective data that are less susceptible to respondent bias than survey data.

Records of all complaints about reference services can be logged, entered into a database, and then analyzed. In using complaints or any other type of existing data, you must consider the original reason for collecting the data, what the data may actually be measuring, and whether the data were collected consistently. For instance, we know that complaint data would not be a good way to measure general satisfaction with reference service, but it might be quite useful in identifying some of the major reasons for user dissatisfaction.

We also know, however, that many users who are dissatisfied do not complain, so we could not be certain that the complaints were representative of dissatisfied users as a whole (Hirschman 1970).

DESIGNING AN OBSERVATIONAL STUDY

If you have determined that your assessment requires the collection of data related to behavior, you will definitely want to include a method for collecting observational data as part of your study. As a first step, you should review the annotations for the observational studies included in the chapter 5 section of the "Reference Assessment Annotated Bibliography" in this book. These studies provide excellent guides for replicating an observational technique. By reviewing the ways that study findings were used to evaluate and change reference services, these studies can also assist you in determining which observational method might be most appropriate for your study goals.

Once you have selected the most appropriate observational method, you will need to develop an observational form to collect the data. A form for observations is important to ensure reliability and validity of observations. The form will ensure that for each observation the same type of information is recorded. The form also allows the researcher to determine what sort of data will be collected on each event that is observed.

Data analysis methods should be planned during this time. Observational forms can be designed to make processing the data for analysis more efficient. If you have your data analysis strategy planned in advance and design your data collection form appropriately, you can save considerable time when entering data into the Statistical Package for the Social Sciences (SPSS), Ethnograph, Nudist, or other similar software programs that support the quantitative or qualitative analysis of data. (For additional information on the SPSS, Ethnograph, and Nudist, you can consult the website for SPSS at http://www. spss.com and the website for The Ethnograph and QSR NUD*IST at http://www.scolari.com.) If you have not had any experience with data analysis, at this stage of the project you should consult with someone who has some experience. Experts can be located through professional associations, nearby universities, or by contacting people who have done research in the field using similar data-collection methods. You can use the chapter 5 section in the "Reference Assessment Annotated Bibliography" to identify some of the experienced researchers in the field. Most researchers are generous with their time and are very willing to provide some basic advice. Researchers who believe in the value and importance of assessment projects want to assist and encourage others to do evaluation studies of reference services.

After you have developed an observational form and reviewed it for efficient data analysis, you need to field test the form before actually collecting the data for your study. You will find that no discussion with or review by colleagues can replace the experience of pilot testing the draft observation form in the field. After each observation session, time should be allowed to fully develop notes and to reflect upon patterns and gaps in the data collected. You will also want to continue this practice after each observation session once you have begun the actual study.

Besides pilot testing and revising the preliminary observation form, you must develop a plan for sampling the events you wish to observe. The sampling plan should ensure that you observe the full range and variety of events in order to represent the entire population that you intend to sample. Again, if you do not have any experience with sampling, you should consult someone who can advise you on how to select a sample. People who can provide technical assistance with data analysis should also be able to help you design a sampling plan. Sampling in reference observation studies is often concerned with sampling reference interactions at different times of the day to ensure that questions from a wide range of patrons using the library on nights, weekends, afternoons, and mornings are included in the sampled observations.

You should also design the sampling plan to collect observations in such a way as to eliminate any systematic bias. For example, selecting every fifth person who approaches a catalog workstation decreases the potential for bias. Beepers can also ensure that times for observations are randomly selected (Spencer 1980). If observers do not have some systematic plan, they may be likely to approach people who look more attractive or friendly, or who perhaps look like themselves! These individuals might not behave in the same way that people who look less approachable would behave. If this were true, you might introduce unintended bias into your study.

ETHICAL ISSUES

Much of the controversy surrounding unobtrusive studies concerns ethical issues. To avoid contaminated results related to changes in behavior when people know they are being observed, unobtrusive studies are conducted without the knowledge of people participating in the event.

The first ethical rule in research is to do no harm to the participants. Another way to state this rule is to ask: does my project put participants at risk of harm? The highest standard to avoid harm to participants is to provide a statement of "informed consent" to participants. Under the "informed consent" standard, participants have an opportunity to review and sign a statement that tells them the purpose of the research. Informed consent statements must also assure people that their participation in the research is voluntary, that withdrawal or refusal to participate will have no harmful consequences for them, and that personal information will be kept confidential. Participants should also be given the name and contact information for a person who will answer questions about the project.

Unobtrusive studies do not meet the highest standard of informed consent because participants do not know that they are being observed. Generally, observations take place in a public setting, and the act of observing may not violate people's right to privacy because the general public has a right to observe the performance of reference librarians or others in public service roles. Even if this is so, a central ethical concern should be protecting participants from the risk of harm. Researchers should restrict access to all information that might reveal people's identities. When transcripts are made from tapes or observation notes are completed, names and specific information which have the potential to identify individual participants, such as physical descriptions, very detailed demographic information, or identifying events and places, should be removed or modified.

Observations have the potential to put participants at significant risk if observers report the identity of staff members they observed to librarian supervisors or others responsible for evaluations, promotions, or pay increases. In a broader sense, unobtrusive evaluations, if undertaken without the informed consent of reference department members, may do harm to the morale and self-esteem of reference librarians and staff, even if results related to the performance of individual members are not revealed.

SUMMARY

Observation is most valuable when collecting information on behavior is essential for meeting the goals of your evaluation project. Observation methods provide a more reliable measure of how people actually behave than data collected through surveys, focus groups, or interviews. In planning a study, the use of a wide range of observation techniques should be considered, including direct observation, observers disguised as patrons, self-observation, recording devices, physical traces, and existing data.

Using a carefully designed form to collect the observational data most appropriate to your study goals will help ensure that the data are reliable and valid. Issues related to sampling, data analysis, and the protection of the rights of human subjects need to be carefully considered when you plan your project. Pilot testing of your observation technique is also essential. For readers interested in utilizing observation methods, the chapter 5 section of the "Reference Assessment Annotated Bibliography" provides an invaluable supplement to this brief overview.

Works Cited

Arrigona, D., and E. Mathews. 1988. A use study of an academic library reference collection. *RQ* 28: 71–81.

Crews, K. D. 1988. The accuracy of reference service. *Library and Information Science Research* 10: 331–355.

Crowley, T., and T. A. Childers. 1971. *Information service in public libraries: Two studies.* Metuchen, N.J.: Scarecrow.

Evaluation of Reference and Adult Services Committee (ERASC). Reference and Adult Services Division. American Library Association. 1995. *Reference assessment manual.* Ann Arbor: Pierian.

Hernon, P., and C. R. McClure. 1987. *Unobtrusive testing and library reference services.* Norwood, N.J.: Ablex.

Hirschman, A. O. 1970. *Exit, voice, and loyalty.* Cambridge, Mass.: Harvard Univ. Pr.

Hunter, R. 1991. Successes and failures of patrons searching the online catalog at a large academic library: A transaction log analysis. *RQ* 30: 395–402.

Ingwersen, P. 1982. Search procedures in the library—analyzed from the cognitive point of view. *Journal of Documentation* 38: 165–191.

Kazlauskas, E. 1976. An exploratory study: A kinesic analysis of academic library public service points. *Journal of Academic Librarianship* 2: 130–134.

King, G. 1982. Try it—you'll like it: A comprehensive management information system for reference services. *Reference Librarian,* no. 3: 71–78.

Kuhlthau, C. C. 1988a. Developing a model of the library search process: Cognitive and affective aspects. *RQ* 28: 232–242.

Kuhlthau, C. C. 1988b. Longitudinal case studies of the information search process of users in libraries. *Library and Information Science Research* 10: 257–304.

Kuhlthau, C. C. 1988c. Perceptions of the information search process in libraries: A study of changes from high school through college. *Information Processing & Management* 24: 419–427.

Lynch, M. J. 1978. Reference interviews in public libraries. *Library Quarterly* 48: 119–142.

Peters, T. A. 1989. When smart people fail: An analysis of the transaction log of an online public access catalog. *Journal of Academic Librarianship* 15: 267–273.

Spencer, C. C. 1980. Random time sampling. *Bulletin of the Medical Library Association* 68: 53–57.

Von Seggern, M. 1989. Evaluating the interview. *RQ* 29: 260–265.

Weech, T. L., and H. Goldhor. 1982. Obtrusive versus unobtrusive evaluation of reference service in five Illinois public libraries: A pilot study. *Library Quarterly* 52: 305–324.

Welch, J. M., L. A. Cauble, and L. B. Little. 1997. Automated reshelving statistics as a tool in reference collection management. *Reference Services Review: RSR* 25: 79–85.

6

Individual Interviews
and Focus Group Interviews

This chapter provides an overview of the use of individual interviews and group interviews (focus groups) and their value to reference evaluation projects. The topics covered include when to use interviews rather than other assessment methods; how to plan interview studies; the use of structured and unstructured interviews and focus groups; the design of interview studies; and ethical issues. This chapter is intended to supply the basic information you need to decide whether interviews will be useful as part of your project. The chapter 6 section of the "Reference Assessment Annotated Bibliography" contains summaries of reference studies that use interviews. These studies provide excellent guides when you are planning an interview study. For focus group interviewing, an excellent practical guide is the *Focus Group Kit* (Morgan and Krueger 1997).

WHAT ARE INTERVIEWS, AND WHY WOULD
I WANT TO CONDUCT THEM?

Interviews and focus groups require more time than surveys and questionnaires but are a richer source of information. Interviews are the best method for understanding how people interpret their world, describe their experiences, and articulate their attitudes, perspectives, concerns, and values. Interviews provide a valuable supplement to observational data on people's behavior and interaction with their environment. Interviews can also assist you in interpreting observational data. For example, what is it about the reference desk that makes people reluctant to approach? What perspectives and experiences underlie the behavior of people who do or don't use reference services?

Because of the expense and time required, interviews are not a cost-effective method for collecting the opinions and attitudes of large groups of people. Higher administrative costs are related to scheduling participant interviews and the careful training of staff who will be conducting the interviews.

Interviews are valuable in the early stages of designing questionnaires, but they are also very valuable after surveys have been completed. Once questionnaire findings have been reviewed, you may have questions on why people responded as they did. You might find, for example, that people are highly satisfied with reference service but reported a fairly low success rate in finding the information they needed. While the survey data cannot tell you why participants gave these apparently conflicting responses, in-depth interviews of a limited number of respondents might provide one or more possible answers.

GETTING STARTED

Once you decide that interviews should be part of your project, careful planning of the interview procedures will enhance the quality of your study and enable you to make the most effective use of your time. To assist you in this task, sample planning checklists are included for both individual interviews and focus groups (figures 6.1 and 6.2).

Effective planning must include the design of interview questions that are based on your study goals, review and revision of those questions by other colleagues involved in the study, and identification of adequate resources and budget to support your project. Planning should include an outline of the sequence of events, the person responsible for each phase, dates, and costs involved. An essential part of planning is adequate provision for training interviewers or hiring a well-qualified focus group facilitator. You can also expect to devote considerable time to recruiting and scheduling interviews with participants!

FIGURE 6.1
Sample Planning Checklist for Interviews

1. Determine the purpose of the study

   Procedures: _____ review literature; _____ consult colleagues

   Budget and Resources: _____ estimate time required

2. Plan the methods of collecting interview data

   Procedures: _____ evaluate telephone, e-mail, or in-person strategies

   Budget and Resources: _____ estimate time required;

   _____ estimate costs of each strategy

3. Conduct the interviews based upon an interview guide

   Procedures: _____ develop questions and guide; _____ recruit & train interviewers;

   _____ pilot test interview guide; _____ recruit participants;

   _____ identify interview location and equipment

   Budget and Resources: _____ estimate time required;

   _____ fees for participants and interviewers?

4. Transcribe the interview notes

   Procedures: _____ hire an individual to transcribe or do yourself?

   Budget and Resources: _____ obtain transcription equipment;

   _____ estimate time required

5. Analyze the interview material

   Procedures: _____ devise coding scheme; _____ review and code material

   Budget and Resources: _____ obtain computer software?

   _____ estimate time required

6. Verify the findings

   Procedures: _____ others perform coding; _____ draft report of findings;

   _____ colleagues review and comment on findings

   Budget and Resources: _____ estimate time required

7. Communicate the findings

   Procedures: _____ prepare final report

   Budget and Resources: _____ copy expenses

FIGURE 6.2
Sample Planning Checklist for Focus Groups

---

1. Determine the purpose of the study

     Procedures: _____ review the literature; _____ consult colleagues

     Budget and Resources: _____ estimate time required

2. Develop questions and prepare a guide

     Procedures: _____ review literature; _____ consult colleagues; _____ draft guide

     Budget and Resources: _____ estimate time required

3. Identify participants, types of characteristics

     Procedures: _____ develop potential participant pool

     Budget and Resources: _____ estimate time required

4. Identify facilitator and note taker

     Procedures: _____ identify potential facilitators or train people as facilitators

     Budget and Resources: _____ estimate time required;

     _____ pay facilitators or pay for training people to facilitate

5. Pilot test questions

     Procedures: _____ recruit volunteers

     Budget and Resources: _____ obtain room and equipment;

     _____ estimate time required

6. Recruit participants

     Procedures: _____ contact and obtain consent; _____ schedule

     Budget and Resources: _____ estimate time required

7. Conduct focus groups and record sessions

     Procedures: _____ send reminder notices

     Budget and Resources: _____ schedule room;

     _____ arrange for equipment, e.g., flip charts, recorders;

     _____ arrange for food and other incentives, e.g., pay

8. Transcribe the focus group interviews

     Procedures: _____ hire someone to transcribe or do yourself;

     Budget and Resources: _____ estimate time required;

     _____ obtain transcription equipment

9. Analyze the focus group material

  Procedures: _____ review, analyze patterns, and code material

  Budget and Resources: _____ estimate time required;
  _____ obtain computer software?

10. Review and revise draft of findings

  Procedures: _____ colleagues and others involved in study review draft

  Budget and Resources: _____ estimate time required

11. Communicate the findings

  Procedures: _____ prepare final report

  Budget and Resources: _____ copy expenses

In planning your study, you should be concerned about the validity, or truth and correctness, and reliability, or consistency, of the interview data. Validity is related to how trustworthy the reports of the respondents are and how accurately the material is transcribed. Respondents should have an opportunity to review and comment upon material that has been transcribed. The interpretations and conclusions drawn from the data should be based on sound logic.

For interview data, reliability issues are related to consistency—for example, when respondents are asked different questions, are their responses consistent? If an individual responds by indicating that she asked a reference question once a week at the desk and then indicates that this is the first time she has ever used the library, these responses clearly require follow-up questions! An important procedure for enhancing reliability is to plan to have more than one individual code the interview data during the analysis. This check will make certain the material is consistently coded across all interviews.

SELECTION OF AN INTERVIEW METHOD

Structured and unstructured individual interviews or focus group interviews can all provide valuable information for projects utilizing interview methods. To assist you in determining which method might be most appropriate for your study goals, each form of interview is reviewed. Examples of reference studies using these methods are also provided.

Structured and Unstructured Interviews

A structured interview is led by the interviewer. Questions are predetermined. Both closed and open-ended questions can be utilized effectively in the structured interview. Closed questions give respondents a choice from a set of answers offered by the researcher and thus suggest to people how they ought to respond. Responses can not only be influenced by the predetermined categories; they can also be limited by choices that are not offered to respondents. Open-ended questions allow respondents to provide their own answers, unbiased by the researcher's questions or preconceived notions. Figure 6.3 includes examples of both closed and open-ended questions.

FIGURE 6.3

Sample Questions from Interview Schedule for Participants
in Study of Information-Seeking Behavior*

Thank you for your participation in this study. Please answer the following questions about your background. All information provided by you for the purpose of this study will remain strictly confidential.

Part I

Name:

Sex: Male/Female

Age:

Major:

Specialization:

Previous Education:

Desired Career Degree:

Part II

I. Please tell me about your area of concentration. Can you describe it for me in some detail?

II. Do the instructors in your field require you to use the library? If so, where do you go to get help and why? Do you seek a specific area or person?

III. Have you ever had occasion to use the archives or special collections department? If so, what kinds of materials did you use there?

V. Now I want to talk about preparation for term projects.

    a) Do you use primary sources? _____ Yes _____ No _____ Sometimes

    b) Secondary sources? _____ Yes _____ No _____ Sometimes

    c) How do you find these sources? (Please circle statements that apply)

        1. Tracing references in secondary sources

        2. Talking with colleagues

        3. Talking with adviser

        4. Talking with other instructors

        5. Talking with librarians

        6. Using bibliographies

        7. Using library catalogs

          Which ones?_____

    d) In preparing term projects, how do you know when you have found enough information for your work?

VIII. Please comment on the impact (if any) the expansion of use of electronic technology has had on your field of study.

IX. Have you ever done a bibliographic database search? _____ Yes _____ No

    Has someone ever done a bibliographic database search for you? _____ Yes _____ No

    a) Do you seek the help of librarians for your research? _____ Yes _____ No

        _____ Sometimes

    b) Is ORION, the library's online catalog, useful to you? _____ Yes _____ No

        _____ Sometimes

    Are there other online services useful to you? If so, please describe them.

XIII. How do you decide what library (ies) you will use? Do you make judgments about the quality of the libraries you use, and how do you do that? What distinguishes the best libraries from the worst?

---

*Instrument has not been published and was obtained, with permission to reproduce selected questions, from R. Delgadillo and B. P. Lynch. Results of the study using the instrument are reported in R. Delgadillo and B. P. Lynch, "Future Historians: Their Quest for Information," *College & Research Libraries* 60 (1999): 245–59.

The one-minute paper is a common classroom assessment technique that uses open-ended questions as a means of gaining feedback from students. This technique allows course revisions in order to maximize student learning in the middle of the course. The one-minute paper can easily be adapted for use in reference services in order to obtain feedback from patrons on a continuous basis. Figure 6.4 provides a sample "one-minute paper" for reference services.

An interview guide should be constructed for both structured and unstructured interviews. You should begin the interview guide with an outline of topics to be covered. In structured interviews, the main questions should ask for descriptions of experience. Questions on descriptions of experience can be followed by "how" questions, for example: "How did you feel when you approached the reference desk?"

The number of questions should produce interviews long enough to collect the essential data, but still consider the time of the respondent. Face-to-face interviews capture the greatest amount of data, including the opportunity to observe nonverbal behavior. Telephone interviews reduce the interviewer effect and possible bias related to nonverbal communication, but their non-response rates will probably be higher. The limitations of telephone interviewing are also related to the difficulty of accessing members of the population who do not have a telephone or have an unlisted number. The length of a phone interview may need to be limited to 15 or 20 minutes. Telephone interviews will be most successful when people have already agreed to participate in the survey.

E-mail interviews reduce the interviewer effect and any possible bias created by the presence of the interviewer. However, the anonymity

FIGURE 6.4
The One-Minute Paper Adapted to the Reference Interview

1. What is the most important thing you learned by using the reference service today?

2. What questions do you still have about the subject (or database)?

3. What important question remains unanswered?

4. Any comments or suggestions?

of respondents' identity cannot be guaranteed. Another difficulty is that all of the participants must have easy access to the Internet. Response rates may also be lower. E-mail interviewing should be considered only when collecting data on nonverbal communication is not important for your project.

Structured interview guides generally consist of main questions that break the subject of the interview into specific parts. This organization sets the broad outline for the interview. Main questions should be developed after a review of the literature. Pilot interviews should be conducted to further refine the questions.

Open-ended questions can be asked about stages in a process, respondents' perceptions about the contributing causes to an outcome, the role of different people participating in the process, what worked well in the process, and what appeared to be unsatisfactory. When respondents describe the process, probes, which encourage respondents to expand upon an answer, can be utilized effectively. Respondents can be asked to put events they are describing in order, to describe their opinions, to provide more factual detail, or to complete an earlier comment. Probes can also be used to return the conversation to the main topic of the interview. They are also useful in determining what respondents know firsthand, as opposed to experiences reported to them by other people. Follow-up questions can be used as part of the interview process to explore new directions or to test answers that appear to contradict information provided by the respondent earlier in the interview.

Use of the critical incident technique for collecting interview data on successful and unsuccessful reference experiences has yielded useful information (Radford 1996; Wilson, Starr-Schneidkraut, and Cooper 1989; ERASC 1995). Figure 6.5 provides examples of open-ended questions used as part of the critical incident technique to determine patterns of effective and ineffective reference service.

Focus Group Interviews

Focus groups are a form of group interviewing. They are different from individual interviews because focus groups emphasize the interaction between participants. Focus groups provide a unique opportunity for people to influence each other in forming, revising, and

FIGURE 6.5

Sample Questions for Collecting Data on Critical Incidents for Reference Services

---

For Successful Experiences:

1. Can you think of an instance in which the information you obtained from the reference desk was especially helpful to you?

2. What was the situation which led you to ask this question at the reference desk?

3. What specific information were you seeking?

4. What information did you obtain as a result of your query?

5. How did the reference assistance help you?

For Unsuccessful Experiences:

1. Can you think of an experience in which the information you received from the reference desk was unsatisfactory or not helpful to you?

2. In what way was the response from the reference desk unsatisfactory?

3. What response would have been more helpful to you?

4. What was the result of not having a satisfactory response?

---

articulating their views, and in sharing and reflecting upon similar and different experiences. Focus groups must be carefully planned and designed to obtain the participants' views on how they regard an idea, event, experience, or organization.

Historically, the most common focus group applications have been in business as part of market research for product enhancement or new product development. In recent years, nonprofit groups have become much more aware of the need to regularly seek feedback from the clientele they serve. Focus group applications are also becoming more common in assessing services. Professionals, who provide services, can obtain valuable information about user perspectives, beliefs, feelings, and views. Massey-Burzio (1998) has provided a good description of important information that can be collected from focus groups and used in evaluating reference services (figure 6.6).

Focus groups are often used in the early stages of projects and are followed by other research methods. Focus groups can be used to explore research topics, develop questions, and clarify concepts to be used for questionnaires or in-depth interviews. Focus groups can also be useful in the final stages of research projects, for example, to interpret puzzling survey results by obtaining in-depth explanations and responses from a small number of respondents.

Focus groups are also an important method when used alone. They are most useful when surveys or individual interviews are difficult because a population is hard to reach. For example, focus groups on the perspectives of nonusers of reference services can be conducted in certain organizational settings where library use is thought to be low.

Focus groups provide real-life perspectives in a social environment and get quick results. You can collect more data in a shorter amount of time than in individual interviews. Focus groups are rel-

FIGURE 6.6
Information Sought from Focus Group Participants*

Descriptions of experiences in retrieving information in the library, including the kinds of problems participants had and what they did when they ran into a problem

How participants learned to use the library

What participants thought of the staff at the service desk—did they ask them questions, did they like to ask questions? What did participants utilize the staff for and what was the experience like?

How participants felt about their skill in using the library

What participants did not know

What value participants placed on learning to use the library

*From V. Massey-Burzio, "From the Other Side of the Reference Desk: A Focus Group Study," *Journal of Academic Librarianship* 24 (1998): 208–215.

atively low in cost compared to individual interviews and observational techniques. Focus groups are valuable not only for obtaining different perspectives and shared understandings of everyday life, but also for determining the degree of consensus on a topic.

However, recruiting and scheduling participants for focus groups can be very challenging. Moreover, trained facilitators are essential. Facilitators must be skilled in leadership and interpersonal communication, especially listening and non-judgmental techniques. Being a facilitator can be particularly challenging when certain people tend to dominate the discussion. Focus group data are more difficult to summarize than survey data. Focus group results cannot be assumed to represent a larger population because of the small total numbers involved in most studies, and the probability that the participants will not be randomly selected from the population as a whole.

Questions to guide and focus the discussion must be prepared in advance. The number of questions should be limited—six to twelve questions are recommended. Questions should start with more general topics, followed by more specific queries. Figures 6.7 through 6.9 contain focus group questions from reference and information-seeking studies. The focus group questions in figure 6.7 were used to test the hypothesis that an increasing level of anxiety regularly expressed by the reference desk staff appeared to be correlated with an increase in end-users' access to electronic resources. The questions in figure 6.8 were designed to learn more about the information-seeking needs of young residents of San Mateo County; focus groups were conducted in a YMCA "teens at high risk" group, a local middle school, and a high school.

In organizing and recruiting focus groups, the number of focus groups you should conduct depends upon the topic. For your first study you should start with two or three focus groups, analyze the results of each session, and then decide if you should conduct additional sessions. Although ten to twelve people in each focus group session was once the standard number, the trend today is toward smaller groups of five to eight participants. Smaller groups facilitate greater in-depth discussions, with each participant having an opportunity to take part more fully. Smaller groups are also less difficult to schedule, easier to moderate, more comfortable for participants, and

FIGURE 6.7

Focus Group Questions for Assessing Technostress at the Reference Desk*

1. What do you enjoy most about working at the reference desk?

2. Describe your ideal hour working at the reference desk.

3. How does your real experience match the ideal? Follow-up: How do you counter your frustration?

4. Imagine yourself at the reference desk. The phone rings. Describe the encounter.

5. Your job today is to paint the reference desk and everything on it. What colors will you use?

6. If a genie came out of a lamp and gave you three wishes, what would you change about your work at the reference desk? Follow-up: What is the best way to learn the new technology?

7. Fill in speech "bubbles" for this picture [picture of two women—both standing—one behind the desk, more formally dressed; the other, more casually dressed, in front of the desk].

8. If a genie of the reference desk lamp could teach you one thing about working the reference desk, what would it be?

*From P. M. Rose, K. Stoklosa, and S. A. Gray, "A Focus Group Approach to Assessing Technostress at the Reference Desk," *Reference & User Services Quarterly* 37 (1998): 311–317.

permit more group homogeneity. Group homogeneity is generally desirable because people will feel more comfortable, although homogeneity also tends to limit the diversity of views expressed.

Focus group participants are composed of people who have something in common. You will want to select focus group participants based on the purpose of the study. For focus groups you don't want random sampling, but instead want to select people who have special knowledge or experiences that will be helpful in your study. You can also assemble a larger pool of qualified participants and then select randomly from that pool.

Focus group sessions should be conducted by two moderators. During the actual session, one moderator, who should be a trained and skilled facilitator, introduces the topic, asks the questions, and

FIGURE 6.8
Focus Group Questions for San Mateo Public Library*

1. What are some of the fun activities you like to do?

2. Do you participate in any clubs, groups, or church activities?

3. What types of activities do you like to do with your family? Your friends?

4. When you need information, how do you go about finding information?

5. Do you speak other languages, besides English?

6. Do any of you use the library and if so, have you used it in the last year?

7. If you were in charge of the library and wanted to attract people in your age group, what would you do?

8. If you have not used the library, can you tell me why?

---

*Questions developed as part of the Needs Assessment Project for the San Mateo Public Library, San Mateo, Calif., by Armando Ramirez and Jo Bell Whitlatch.

---

facilitates the group discussion, while the other moderator records nonverbal communication, monitors the tape recording, and clarifies issues by taking notes on flip charts. Sessions should begin with a brief introduction of the facilitator and recorder and a summary of the purpose of the session. Focus groups should be planned for sixty to ninety minutes. Food or some other small gift of appreciation for the participants will encourage participation.

ETHICAL ISSUES

The first rule in collecting data from subjects is to do no harm to the participants. As part of conducting research, you must establish procedures that protect participants from risk. For individual interviews, a good practice is to begin by asking the subject to review and sign a written statement of informed consent. *Informed consent* means that

FIGURE 6.9
Complaint System Questions*

1. Can you remember a time when you were very pleased with reference service? It could have been in an academic, public, or more specialized library, and you felt good about what happened. Tell us about it.

2. Think about the last time you complained about the reference service you received. Tell us what happened.

3. Have you ever thought about complaining but decided not to say anything? Tell us about it.

4. Think about reference service complaints in libraries and in business organizations. Are complaints handled differently?

5. Think about your experiences with (name of library). Have you ever complained or thought about making a complaint? Tell us about it.

6. Has anyone ever complained to you about some service or product you provided? What did you do about the complaint?

7. For this next question, you'll need this piece of paper. Pretend that we're putting together a report card for (name of library). Think about categories of complaints. What categories would be needed for the report card? Write the possible categories on the paper.
   WAIT A FEW MINUTES FOR PARTICIPANTS TO COMPLETE THEIR LISTS.
   OK, let's list your categories on the flip chart.

8. How do we encourage people or make them feel it's all right to give us feedback or make complaints?

9. When we receive a complaint, what should be done about it?

10. What does "resolving a complaint" mean to you?

11. Think about all that we have talked about today. What do you think is most important for (name of library) to keep doing?

12. Was the summary adequate? Have we missed anything?

---

*Adapted from R. A. Krueger, "Developing Questions for Focus Groups," *Focus Group Kit,* ed. D. L. Morgan and R. A. Krueger, vol. 3 (Thousand Oaks, Calif.: Sage, 1997).

the participant understands the nature of the research and has voluntarily agreed to participate in it. The informed consent statement should advise the subject of the purpose of the research, the nature of information to be requested during the interview, and provide guarantees of the privacy and confidentiality of individual responses. The statement also needs to explain that participation in the interview is voluntary and that withdrawal or refusal to participate will not result in any adverse consequences, such as limiting services provided by the library to the individual.

The participants in interviews must be able to freely share their experiences and opinions with the assurance that the information will not be used against them. Access to tape recordings and transcripts of individual interviews should be restricted. Once your project is completed, transcripts and recordings of individual interviews should be destroyed. When individual interviews are summarized, names and other information that could reveal identity must be deleted or modified.

Focus groups are not fully confidential, because comments are shared with everyone participating in the discussion. For this reason, focus groups should not contain a mix of employees and supervisors or other combinations that involve some individuals who have power and authority over others in their group. Typically, focus groups are tape recorded, but you must request permission for tape recording from all participants. Although participants should be encouraged to keep discussions confidential, focus groups are generally not the best method for collecting sensitive personal information or perspectives on highly controversial topics.

SUMMARY

Interviews and focus groups provide the best method for understanding how people interpret the world through their experiences, perspectives, thoughts, and feelings. Interview methods include individual interviews that are structured or unstructured and group interviews that require a structured and focused discussion guide.

Works Cited

Delgadillo, R., and B. P. Lynch. 1999. Future historians: Their quest for information. *College & Research Libraries* 60: 245–259.

Krueger, R. A. 1997. Developing questions for focus groups. In *Focus group kit,* ed. D. L. Morgan and R. A. Krueger. Vol. 3. Thousand Oaks, Calif.: Sage.

Massey-Burzio, V. 1998. From the other side of the reference desk: A focus group study. *Journal of Academic Librarianship* 24: 208–215.

Morgan, D. L., and R. A. Krueger, eds. 1997. *Focus group kit.* Thousand Oaks, Calif.: Sage.

Radford, M. L. 1996. Communication theory applied to the reference encounter: An analysis of critical incidents. *Library Quarterly* 66: 123–137.

Rose, P. M., K. Stoklosa, and S. A. Gray. 1998. A focus group approach to assessing technostress at the reference desk. *Reference & User Services Quarterly* 37: 311–317.

Wilson, S. R., N. Starr-Schneidkraut, and M. D. Cooper. 1989. *Use of the critical incident technique to evaluate the impact of MEDLINE (final report).* Palo Alto, Calif.: American Institute for Research in the Behavioral Sciences. The instrument used to evaluate the impact of MEDLINE is available in Evaluation of Reference and Adult Services Committee, Reference and Adult Services Division. American Library Association. 1995. *Reference assessment manual.* Ann Arbor: Pierian.

7

Case Studies

This chapter provides an overview of the use of case studies in evaluating reference services. The topics covered include when to use the case study method, how to plan case studies, the design of case studies, and ethical issues. This chapter should provide you with sufficient information to decide whether the case study approach is the best one for your project. The chapter 7 section of the "Reference Assessment Annotated Bibliography" contains summaries of case studies in the reference environment. These case studies supplement this brief introduction and will assist you in planning your own case study.

WHAT IS A CASE STUDY, AND WHY WOULD I WANT TO CONDUCT ONE?

A case study is an in-depth study of a limited number of situations or environments. By using a combination of assessment methods, such as interviews, observations, and surveys, a rich description of a small number of environments can be developed. This enables you to analyze the patterns and typical situations within one environment or a limited number of situations.

Case studies do have important limitations. Usually, the findings from a case study cannot be applied to other situations. Case studies, however, can be conducted in two or more similar situations or environments, or, after a case study is completed, the case study methods can be replicated in another organization.

In the reference environment, case studies can be particularly valuable for assessing new reference services or products and current reference operations in order to improve the quality of services to users. The combination of methods typically used in case studies can provide a more reliable and valid study than single assessment methods in one or two reference settings. Each assessment method has its different strengths and limitations. This is why a well-designed and carefully planned case study can be so useful: it provides an assessment that is far superior to a single user survey of reference service successes and failures.

When using the case study approach, important techniques to enhance the validity, or truth and correctness, of the data collected are to

1. Use multiple sources of evidence; for example, self-reports of both users and librarians, independent observers of the reference encounter, and existing data (e.g., transaction logs) from online or other electronic databases.
2. Have at least some study participants and colleagues, who are involved in the project, review the draft report.
3. Develop explanations that conflict with each other and collect information to support or reject both explanations.
4. Replicate the case study in a similar environment or situation.

In case study research you also need to be concerned about the reliability, or consistency, of the data. Important techniques to enhance reliability are to

1. Develop formal study questions.
2. Use formal procedures and rules to follow when collecting the data.
3. Develop a case study database with notes and evidence integrated from each assessment method and organized to address each research topic or question.

GETTING STARTED

Planning your study is essential whenever you are conducting an evaluation project. Good case studies use a variety of evidence collected not only from different sources, but through a variety of assessment methods. Therefore, the planning involved in selecting and coordinating the collection of the various types of data can be especially challenging. You should include an outline of the sequence of events, designate a person responsible for each phase of the project, and specify the dates of project phases and the costs involved for each phase. Figure 7.1 provides a planning checklist to help you organize and plan a case study.

DESIGNING THE CASE STUDY

Case studies rely on multiple sources for evidence and the establishment of facts. An important concept underlying the design of effective case studies is triangulation—a fact may be considered established if evidence from three or more sources confirms it. For case studies in the reference environment, the potential sources of evidence include users; library staff; third-party observers of user or library staff behavior and interactions; transaction logs or other types of evidence collected as part of regular library operations, and documentation or archival sources created for another reason. The assessment methods most commonly used in case studies are interviews, including

FIGURE 7.1
Sample Case Study Planning Checklist

---

1. Develop research questions, including conflicting explanations

    Procedures: _____ review literature; _____ consult with colleagues

    Budget and Resources: _____ estimate time required;

                        _____ travel funds to visit other case study sites?

2. Identify potential sources for collecting evidence

    Procedures: _____ survey all possible sources for collecting data

    Budget and Resources: _____ estimate time required

3. Determine assessment methods

    Procedures: _____ review strengths, limitations, of all possible methods;

    _____ review study goals and determine most appropriate measures

    Budget and Resources: _____ estimate time required

4. For each assessment method, design instruments to collect data

    Procedures: _____ consult with case study researchers;

    _____ pilot test all instruments;

    _____ revise instruments as needed

    Budget and Resources: _____ copying and distributing instruments;

    _____ fees for expert consultants;

    _____ fees for participants

5. Schedule and coordinate the collection of case study data

    Procedures: _____ train interviewers or surveyors; _____ recruit respondents

    Budget and Resources: _____ prepare detailed timeline for all data-collection phases;

    _____ copying and distributing instruments;

    _____ fees for participants

6. Organize and analyze case study data

    Procedures: _____ coding; _____ data entry; _____ create case study database;

    _____ identify patterns; _____ draft report;

    _____ circulate draft report; _____ revise draft report

    Budget and Resources: _____ data entry support; _____ computer software;

    _____ estimate time required

7. Communicate case study findings

    Procedures: _____ present final report in writing and orally

    Budget and Resources: _____ copying expenses

focus groups; observations; surveys; and the analysis of existing documents or records.

A well-designed case study should include evidence from a variety of sources collected through the use of different assessment methods. The sources and methods you choose to use in your case study will depend upon your evaluation project goals. To help you decide, certain published case studies provide good examples of how different methods and sources have been used in combination to assess reference services. The chapter 7 section of the "Reference Assessment Annotated Bibliography" summarizes several case studies completed in a reference environment. In addition, table 7.1 summarizes the goals, methods, and sources utilized in these case studies.

When you are designing your case study, remember that

1. Surveys are most useful in collecting opinions, attitudes, views, and perceptions from a large number of respondents.
2. Interviews are best for understanding the real-life world, self-perceptions, and experiences of a more limited number of respondents.
3. Observations are most useful in understanding how people actually behave as opposed to how they say they would behave.

ETHICAL ISSUES

As noted in previous chapters, the first rule of conducting research involving human subjects is to do no harm to the participants. The ethical safeguards discussed in the previous chapters on surveys, observations, interviews, and focus groups also apply when these methods are used in combination in a case study. In addition, when the evidence from all sources is summarized and organized under each topic or research question, you should check your draft report carefully to make certain that the privacy and confidentiality of all individual respondents are respected. Names and identifying details may need to be changed to protect the identity of the participants.

SUMMARY

Case studies are in-depth studies of a limited number of situations or environments. They use a variety of techniques from different sources to meet specific study goals. Triangulation, or confirming facts or patterns from three or more different sources, is an important concept. In designing case studies, the strengths of different methods need to be considered in relationship to each other as well as to the project goals. A number of reference case studies have been provided in the chapter 7 section of the "Reference Assessment Annotated Bibliography" to assist you in designing a case study appropriate to your project.

TABLE 7.1

Goals, Methods, and Sources from Reference Case Studies

References and annotations for each case study in the table are entered under the authors' names in the chapter 7 section of the "Reference Assessment Annotated Bibliography."

Case Study Authors:

ENVIRONMENT	GOAL	METHODS	SOURCES
Christensen, Benson, Butler, Hall, and Howard: Brigham Young University	effectiveness of student-worker staffing on the reference desk	observation: unobtrusive surveys	15 staff asking 75 questions library assistants, subject specialists, and students
Davenport, Procter, and Goldenberg: University of Edinburgh, Heriot-Watt University, Napier University	explore types of collaborative academic reference service in a digital library environment	interviews diaries observations: videotaped observation: direct survey	librarians librarians librarians consulting other librarians researchers observing users

(continued)

TABLE 7.1 (continued)

Case Study Authors:

ENVIRONMENT	GOAL	METHODS	SOURCES

Devore-Chew, Roberts, and Smith:
  Brigham Young
  University
	study the impact of nonverbal communication on users' perceptions	experimental method using nonverbal behaviors of librarians
		
		surveys
			librarians
			
			users

Gothberg: public library	effect of verbal and nonverbal communication of the reference librarian on question negotiation and user satisfaction	observation: videotapes of reference librarians who are using approaching and distancing behaviors and language cues surveys	librarians and users users

Herman:
  Brandeis
  University
	evaluate tiered reference service	observation: direct
		
		observation: unobtrusive, telephone: 100 questions
		
		focus group interviews
			librarians doing research consultation
			
			library staff asking questions of graduate-student information-desk worker
			
			faculty, under-graduate and graduate students, and researchers

Kirby:
  Medical College of
  Pennsylvania
	compares end-user with experienced intermediary search results	observation	search results

Case Study Authors:

ENVIRONMENT	GOAL	METHODS	SOURCES

Kuhlthau:
    large eastern
    suburban
    high school
	theory of the
	process of
	searching
	for
	information
		search logs,
		journals of
		feelings/thoughts/
		actions,
		flow charts, time-
		lines, observations,
		short writings about
		topics, and interviews
			high-school students

Kuhlthau, Turock,
George, and Belvin:
    eight school, 7 academic,
    and 6 public libraries
	comparison
	of
	information-
	seeking
	process of
	public library
	adults, college
	and high school
	students
		process surveys,
		perceptions,
		questionnaires, and
		flow charts
			public library adults,
			college students, and
			high-school students

Markham, Stirling, and
Smith:
    Brigham Young
    University
	relationship
	of librarians'
	self-disclosure
	to user
	satisfaction
	and willingness
	to return
		observation:
		experimental
		behavior
		using self-disclosure
		as variable
		
		survey
			librarians
			
			users

Mellon: academic library	explore feelings of first-time undergraduate academic library users	observation: comparative analysis	samples of students' personal writing
Mendelsohn: academic library	explore the parameters of quality reference service	interviews	reference providers and users

(continued)

TABLE 7.1 (continued)

Case Study Authors:

ENVIRONMENT	GOAL	METHODS	SOURCES
Michell and Harris: public library	differing assessments of the reference interview by public librarians and users	observation: videotapes of reference interviews	public librarians and users
Nardi and O'Day: Apple and Hewlett-Packard	examines what reference librarians do (as expert providers of reference services) to begin thinking about intelligent software agents	observation interviews: audiotaping observation: analysis	librarians and clients reference librarians and clients online searches
Nassar: Utica College	examine whether the Brandeis Model of Reference Service is a viable alternative in libraries with smaller staff and user populations	interviews surveys	library staff student assistant and users
Olzak: large southeastern undergraduate library	determine the nature and under-lying causes of reference mistakes	observation interviews	reference transactions between librarians and users reference staff

Case Study Authors:

ENVIRONMENT	GOAL	METHODS	SOURCES

Pinkston:
  Toledo-Lucas
  County Public
  Library
	methods and
	techniques
	used to
	evaluate
	services and
	resources
		surveys
		
		Wisconsin-Ohio
		Reference
		Evaluation
		Program [RTAI]
		
		observation
			users
			
			users and reference
			staff
			
			circulation and usage
			statistics

Puttapithakporn: Indiana University	problems users have when searching a basic reference database	observation: direct surveys interviews	researchers observing users users users

Radford:
  two New Jersey
  academic libraries
	role of non-
	verbal commu-
	nication in
	reference service
	interactions
		observation:
		unobtrusive
		
		interviews
			librarians and users
			
			users

Richardson:
  Question Master,
  a decision-support
  system for routine
  reference questions
	usability
	study of
	Question
	Master's
	biographical
	module
		observation:
		videotaping of
		think aloud
		and actions,
		survey interviews
			Four library staff who
			had worked with
			reference questions
			on a daily basis in
			corporate, public, and
			academic libraries

Saracevic, Kantor, Chamis, and Trivison: DIALOG databases	study several aspects of the process of posing queries and retrieving information from informa- tion systems	surveys, interviews: audiotaped observation: retrieved items	users: academic faculty, graduate students, and industry employees searches and items retrieved

(continued)

TABLE 7.1 (continued)

Case Study Authors:

ENVIRONMENT	GOAL	METHODS	SOURCES
Sjolander and Sjolander: Florida State University, University of West Florida in Pensacola	analyze and compare reference services at two libraries	interviews, surveys, and observations	reference department heads, policy documents
Thorne and Whitlatch: San Jose State University	examine comparative success of students using the online catalog with and without reference assistance	surveys	users
		Wisconsin-Ohio Reference Evaluation Program [RTAI]	users and librarians
		observation	librarians observing users searching the online catalog
		survey and observation: document availability study	users and library materials
Tillotson: University of Toronto Library	Internet destinations of users gaining access through UT Link	survey and focus group interviews	users
		observation	logs of telnet sessions
Tygett, Lawson, and Weessies: Central Missouri State University	assessment of reference services	observation: unobtrusive	marketing student proxies asking librarians questions
		surveys, written reports, and focus group interviews	marketing student proxies

CASE STUDIES

Case Study Authors:

ENVIRONMENT	GOAL	METHODS	SOURCES
Von Seggern: university library	testing application of guidelines to the reference interview for department evaluation	observation: audiotaping, and observer notes	user and librarian reference interactions
		focus group interviews	reference librarians
		Wisconsin-Ohio Reference Evaluation Program [RTAI]	users and librarians

Data Analysis

This chapter reviews key issues related to data analysis and also covers planning for the resources needed to support your data collection and analysis. The first section will cover general information related to resources and support. The second section will address data analysis issues related to surveys, observational techniques, interviews and focus groups, and case studies.

WHAT RESOURCES SHOULD I PLAN
FOR DATA COLLECTION AND ANALYSIS?

In conducting any evaluation, there are always some budgetary surprises. Your study will go much more smoothly if you plan all anticipated costs in advance. The planning checklists in previous chapters of this book can assist you in reducing unpleasant budgetary surprises. Figure 8.1 provides you with a summary of items you should consider when planning the resources needed for your assessment project.

You can expect data collection and analysis to be major cost items in your project—they will require considerable time and often involve obtaining funds to support transcribing and coding the data and perhaps purchasing computer software. For this reason, data analysis procedures must be planned early in your project. These proce-

FIGURE 8.1

Items Related to Costs of Collecting and Analyzing Data

Participants
  method of participant selection
  sample size
  participant incentives

Data collection instruments
  preparation of informed consent forms
  preparation of data collection instruments
  pilot testing

Environment
  site(s) of data collection
  cooperation of organizations or other study sites
  informing the community about the project
  coordination with other ongoing projects at the organization or other study site

Personnel
  need for training and hiring personnel to collect and help prepare the data for analysis

Equipment and Supplies
  data analysis software, transcription equipment, etc.
  report writing and dissemination of results

---

dures should be completely developed by the time you have finished pilot testing and revising your data collection instruments.

SURVEYS

Generally, surveys are designed to be administered to a large number of respondents in order to collect data on people's views, perspectives, attitudes, or opinions. Usually, surveys are also used to sample people who will represent the targeted population as a whole. Most data collected by surveys or questionnaires is quantitative and so can be analyzed easily by computer programs designed to do statistical analysis. The most common computer program used in analyzing survey data is the Statistical Package for the Social Sciences, or SPSS (website at: <http://www.spss.com>).

If you are just starting research using surveys, SPSS has several advantages. It is relatively easy to locate someone at a nearby university with knowledge of SPSS, and SPSS itself publishes basic introductory manuals and guides for beginning users. SPSS does all of the standard statistical analyses and has been frequently used by librarians and others doing survey research. If you plan to use SPSS, you should seek advice from someone who has used SPSS previously and can assist you with formatting the questionnaire, so that the coding and processing of the data can be completed cost effectively.

When using SPSS or other statistical programs, you should keep in mind that most of the numbers used in social science surveys represent abstract concepts rather than precise physical phenomena. You should not assume that you can measure attitudes with the same precision that you can measure differences in temperature! Many advanced statistical procedures assume that you have measurements with scales that have order, and that each measurement in the scale is the same distance apart. But some social science data do not even have order; for example, males and females or adults and teenagers cannot truly be placed in an agreed-upon order! For other scales that have order, such as the degree of satisfaction with reference services, you cannot be certain that the distance between very dissatisfied, dissatisfied, satisfied, and very satisfied is the same distance apart as, for example, each hour in the day. You also cannot be certain that all individuals assign the same meaning to the terms when they check the categories.

Because of this lack of precision in measurement, performing highly sophisticated statistical analysis with these fuzzy, imprecise quantities may not yield meaningful results. Often you would be well advised to use descriptive and very basic statistical procedures, such as chi-square and measures of association, to analyze your data. These basic procedures will assist you in identifying patterns in your data and will often be sufficient for understanding and interpreting the evidence. You may even find that SPSS is too high powered, and that a basic spreadsheet program, which comes as part of many word-processing packages, meets your needs for analysis.

If you have included some open-ended questions in your survey but want to summarize and categorize the responses using a statistical program, you can develop a coding scheme for the responses after you review the answers on the questionnaires. Once you develop the categories, assign a number to represent each category, and include these numbers when you enter and run the numbers using the statistical software. After developing the categories, you should have at least one other person code the questionnaire responses using your categories to make certain that the categories are consistently applied to the responses.

OBSERVATION

Observational techniques are used to study what people actually do. The resulting data often consists of written descriptions of behavior and cannot really be represented by numbers. However, structured observation forms can include categories that are checked as well as open-ended response categories. When observers are using a form in which they check categories, statistical programs, such as SPSS, can be utilized in the same manner as they would be for survey data.

Observational data, such as journals and recordings of reference encounters, should be analyzed using methods similar to that used to analyze interview data. The analysis of interview data is discussed in the next section of this chapter. Also, the chapter 5 section of the "Reference Assessment Annotated Bibliography" summarizes observational studies. These studies provide information on how observational data have been analyzed.

INTERVIEWS AND FOCUS GROUPS

Interviews and focus group data concern participants' views and perceptions of their world. These data should be analyzed as descriptions of experience, by systematically summarizing and organizing those descriptions into categories that explain the world of the respondents. The analysis of interview data is much more time-consuming than the analysis of survey data and some observational data. Figure 8.2 provides the recommended steps for analysis of interview data.

FIGURE 8.2
Recommended Steps for Analysis of Interview Data

1. Look for patterns and themes related to the research topic in the interview material.

2. Develop broad coding categories.

3. Organize data by categories.

4. Review data, revise and refine broad categories, breaking into more specific subcategories.

5. Complete coding of data.

6. Have colleagues or research group independently code at least some of the data.

7. Review for consistency of coding between different individuals.

8. Revise coding based on results of the review.

9. Draft copies of report for colleagues or research group to review.

The analysis of interview data should focus on identifying important themes, and on providing examples of content from the interviews that relate to each theme. If you have recorded entire interview sessions, you will need to decide whether to fully transcribe each session, or to use the tapes to listen carefully and make only an abridged transcript that summarizes the key information from the interviews. Once you have gathered the material for each interview together, you should begin by reviewing the material to identify broad coding categories that represent the important themes from your study. For your initial projects, you should design your questions so that they can serve to focus your analysis on the most important project themes. Generally, the important themes are categories or topics that are of concern to patrons or other groups of interviewees.

Once you have developed a few broad categories, on a second pass through the material, you should develop more specific subcategories that refine the coding scheme. If you are coding from transcribed tapes, you might also want to code pauses or hesitations. You can also develop additional coding categories by participant characteristics, such as gender, age, and level of education. You may also want to consider comparing across categories; for example, do people with scientific queries perceive different barriers to information-seeking than do people with queries in the humanities?

Computer software programs can be useful in coding interview data. Standard programs which have been used frequently for coding interviews are Ethnograph and Nudist (see the website at: http://www.scolari.com). Computer analysis has the advantage of making the coding systematic, providing a formal record that is easy to modify and update. Computer analysis is most valuable when working with complete interview transcripts and large numbers of individual or focus group interviews. However, computer analysis software does require a considerable investment of time and expense. The software must be selected and purchased, and time must be invested in learning how to use it. Computer software programs do not actually do the analysis, but they can save time by assisting you in retrieving appropriately coded segments.

Because you will still need to conduct the analysis, the expense and training time for computer software may not be a worthwhile investment if only a few individual interviews or focus groups are included in your project. If you have only a small amount of interview material, you may find using a basic word-processing program, cutting up copies of typed transcripts, and using colored markers for coding different categories to be the most cost-effective ways to organize your data for analysis.

The analysis of focus group data will proceed much more smoothly if certain procedures are followed during the time you are collecting the data. Figure 8.3 gives tips for facilitating your analysis of focus group data. Making careful arrangements for provision of equipment in advance ensures that you will have a successful session and capture the data you need to conduct the analysis. Assigning identification numbers to participants and asking them to complete a brief survey giving basic demographic information will enable you to code data by important demographic characteristics and look for possible differences in patterns by such characteristics as gender, age, and so on. Keeping a log of which participant is speaking during the discussion will enable you to determine whether repeated mentions of a theme or issue were all by the same individual or are concerns shared by several group members.

FIGURE 8.3

Tips for Collecting Focus Group Data for Analysis

---

1. Use a tape recorder and a flip chart. Have a backup tape recorder available in case of equipment failure.

2. The note taker should assign each focus group participant an identification number (i.e., 1, 2, 3, etc.) and keep a log of the speakers that can be matched later with the recorded transcript of the focus group session.

3. Ask each participant to complete a short written survey that asks for basic demographic information, e.g., gender, race, educational level, etc.

4. Ask a final or summarizing question to determine where participants place their priorities.

5. Offer oral summaries at key times during the session to get participants to verify the accuracy of information or to verify crucial concepts emerging from the discussion.

6. The facilitator and the note taker should use a tape recorder to summarize the main issues and discuss key issues immediately after each focus group session.

7. Gather the tapes of the focus group discussion, the facilitator and note taker's post-focus group discussion, flip chart summaries, and any additional notes taken by the focus group leaders, and begin analysis immediately after each focus group session.

After each focus group is completed, beginning the analysis immediately will enable you to identify emerging themes and any changes you may wish to make in the next focus group you conduct. In beginning the analysis, you should look at each theme and write a descriptive summary of key discussion points. You can also begin to identify quotes that are related to the purpose of the study and provide examples of typical or common participant responses, as well as those that represent the range and diversity of perspectives.

You should begin your first focus group project with a small number of focus groups (two or three) and use just five or six questions. If necessary you can add more groups later. Focus group discussions will result in a tremendous amount of data that will be difficult to analyze. Morgan (1998) estimates four to six hours of transcribing time per focus group session and four to twelve hours for analysis using transcripts or tapes.

CASE STUDIES

Case studies use multiple methods and collect evidence from a variety of sources. You should conduct the analysis using the techniques discussed in this chapter under surveys, observation, or interviews. For case studies, you should create a database and use a computer software program that enables you to summarize, by each major theme or topic, the data that has been collected from various sources by different methods. The database will enable you to make certain that your interpretations for each key theme or topic are based upon analysis of all the evidence you have collected in conducting your case study.

SUMMARY

Adequate budgeting for resources to support data analysis must be done early in the study. Planning for essential resources should be completed, at the latest, during the phase of pilot testing the data collection instruments. Surveys are analyzed using largely quantitative techniques; observational studies rely upon a mix of quantitative and qualitative techniques; individual and focus group studies employ primarily qualitative methods; and case studies tend to use a mix of both quantitative and qualitative methods. Computer software programs are not essential for projects involving small amounts of data, but are invaluable for studies with large amounts of data or for case studies where data has been collected from many sources utilizing different methods.

Work Cited

Morgan, D. L. 1998. The focus group guidebook. In *Focus group kit,* ed. D. L. Morgan and R. A. Krueger. Vol.1. Thousand Oaks, Calif.: Sage.

9

The Evaluation Report and Reference Service Effectiveness

This chapter gives tips on how to communicate and disseminate the results of your evaluation project. The chapter also discusses the importance of considering and implementing changes in reference service practice as a result of your project findings. Examples of practical implications for enhancing reference service practice are provided.

WRITING THE EVALUATION REPORT

When writing the report remember to be clear, brief, and concise! Shorter is better. Continuously ask yourself three questions: (1) How can I present the material in a way that is interesting and understandable to others who have not been very involved in the project? (2) What do I have to say that is important and valuable? and (3) Who is my audience and how can I write the report in their language?

The final report should include the purpose of the study, including context and background provided by the most important and relevant professional literature; study goals and objectives; study methods, collection and analysis of data; and discussion of the results, including limitations of the study, directions for future studies, and practical implications for reference service. Figure 9.1 outlines recommended headings for a typical report.

FIGURE 9.1

Contents of the Evaluation Report

---

1. Cover Page

2. Executive Summary

3. Purpose of Evaluation Project

4. Results or Findings

5. Limitations

6. Recommendations

7. Changes in Reference Policies and Practices
   (include if study was done for a specific organization)

8. Appendixes

One of the most important sections of your written report is the "Executive Summary." Many people may want to know something about your study but not be willing to or have much time to invest in reading about the details. The Executive Summary should be only one or two pages. One page is better. This section should state why the research was conducted, the major conclusions, and main recommendations. The Executive Summary should stand alone. In other words, it should make sense by itself, without having to refer to any other sections of the written report.

The section headed "Purpose of Evaluation Report" should state the purpose, project goals and objectives, the research questions, and methods of collecting and analyzing data. The discussion of the research questions should include a summary of the most significant and relevant literature and relate the development of the research questions to previous research study findings. The description of research methods should provide enough information to allow a reader to replicate the reference evaluation project in a similar environment.

The "Results" or "Findings" section should provide an overview of the main findings, with references to appendixes for tables providing a more detailed report of the results. This section should also include a discussion of reliability, validity, and the extent to which your findings may apply to other organizations. The "Limitations" section should discuss the weaknesses of the study design and recommend additional ways of strengthening future evaluation projects.

REFERENCE SERVICE EFFECTIVENESS

The "Recommendations" section of the report is a very important section. In this section, you should highlight interesting findings that suggest promising directions for future evaluation projects. You should also outline the practical implications of your findings and make a series of recommendations for improving the effectiveness of reference services. These recommendations should be linked directly to your study findings. Figures 9.2 through 9.5 illustrate recommendations to change policies and practices that grew out of the findings from evaluation projects.

Your report should include a section on "Changes in Reference Policies and Practices" if your study was developed for a particular organization. In this section you should include proposals for implementing specific changes in reference service policies and practices within the organization. Your report should also include a proposal with recommendations for people responsible for implementing the changes, recommended implementation procedures and dates, and a timeline for evaluating the impact of the changes once they have been implemented for a certain period of time. Once you have completed and circulated the written report, you will still face the challenging task of getting the organization to implement the changes in reference service policies and practices that you have recommended.

At this stage your early project planning can make a difference in the final implementation phase! Colleagues are more likely to actively support the recommended changes if they have been involved in the initial steps of designing the evaluation project and have had opportunities to review and recommend changes in your draft written report.

Presenting an oral as well as a written report is also a very effective method of building support for your recommended changes in policies and practices. People have different preferences for receiv-

FIGURE 9.2

Changes Made at University of California-Santa Cruz Science Library
as a Result of Study Findings*

Both questionnaires and focus groups were used to obtain student and faculty views of the relative importance of various library services. Following the study, the Science Library staff reviewed the results and observed that improvements were needed in several areas including:

1. Poor quality of copy machines in the Science Library

2. Frustration in the slowness of interlibrary loan services

3. Importance of reserves to undergraduate students

4. E-mail reference service desired by the science faculty

5. Term paper workshops desired by undergraduate students

Changes made in policies and practices were

1. Transfer of Library copy service to University copy center, where better quality machines and skilled technicians would provide the service

2. An experiment to improve interlibrary loan service by allowing faculty, staff, and students to use an online request process to order materials not owned by the Library

3. More actively marketing the availability of electronic reserve materials

4. Implementing an e-mail reference service for faculty, staff, and graduate students

5. Providing several term paper workshops per semester

*From W. Wei, "Rethinking Science Library Services: A User Study at the University of California, Santa Cruz," *Science and Technology Libraries* 15 (1995): 17–42.

ing information that are related to their different learning styles. Some individuals may become interested primarily by reading the written report; others will read little of the written report but may become quite interested by an effective oral presentation; still others may require a combination of written and oral presentations. For oral presentations, develop a new outline which creates opportunities for interactive discussion. Oral communication is an effective but very

THE EVALUATION REPORT AND REFERENCE SERVICE EFFECTIVENESS

FIGURE 9.3
Decreasing Anxiety among Reference Desk Staff*

A focus group was conducted among the staff at the Health Science Library of the State University of New York at Buffalo, specifically with segments of the reference desk staff who seemed to experience the most strain. Since the time of the study, the Reference and Education Services Department has implemented several of the recommendations:

Changes in Reference Policy and Practices

1. Experienced librarians are placed with less experienced staff whenever possible to maximize learning opportunities.

2. Feedback mechanisms and library-wide e-mail list notification provide feedback to staff who refer questions to reference librarians.

3. A revised training program for reference desk staff has been developed, culminating in a test to determine strong points and areas needing reinforcement.

4. Ongoing training in library electronic resources and staff participation in campus technology classes has been supported.

5. The telephone answering system has been restructured according to a customer service model in which all calls are answered and responded to at the circulation desk whenever possible. For reference questions, circulation staff intercom the reference desk or transfer the call to the reference offices.

6. An ongoing in-house training program for new electronic resources is planned.

*From P. M. Rose, K. Stoklosa, and S. A. Gray, "A Focus Group Approach to Assessing Technostress at the Reference Desk," *Reference & User Services Quarterly* 37 (1998): 311–317.

different medium than written communication. You will make a much more effective oral presentation if you take the time to draft a separate presentation that is more informal and interactive. Oral reports that paraphrase written ones may be standard fare at research conferences, but reading a written report will definitely not increase staff support for your project recommendations! In your oral presentation, stick to five or six main points you wish to stress that are related to the changes recommended in reference policies and practices.

FIGURE 9.4

Conditions Necessary for Instituting Successful Two-Tiered Reference Service*

Gannett Memorial Library of Utica College instituted the two-tiered model of reference service in 1994. In order to determine the effectiveness of the model, data were collected using interviews, surveys, and a log of reference questions.

Conditions that appear to be prerequisites for success are

1. Rigorous nonprofessional training which results in a competent first tier

2. Highly motivated librarians committed to the model and its goals

3. Carefully designed physical environment which facilitates referral by and supervision of nonprofessionals

4. A busy library with a high patron-to-staff member ratio where there are enough reference transactions per staff member to warrant the diversion of low-level questions

These conditions do not exist at Gannett Memorial and it would seem advisable for the reference department to consider other more traditional service options.

---

*From A. Nassar, "An Evaluation of the Brandeis Model of Reference Service at a Small Academic Library," *Reference Librarian,* no. 58 (1997): 163–176.

After stimulating interest and support for a serious consideration of your recommendations, you will need to develop proposals and outline strategies to ensure that the recommendations are pursued through appropriate organizational channels. Be prepared to be persistent and pursue your recommendations by sending tactful reminder notices if those responsible for approving reference policy and procedural changes do not get back to you within a reasonable amount of time.

SUMMARY

Writing a clear and concise final report is essential for communicating and disseminating the major findings of your evaluation project. The Executive Summary and the Recommendations sections are par-

FIGURE 9.5
In-Service Training Recommendations*

Detailed accounts provided by 52 users, who visited a public library and asked a question that mattered to them personally, provided the basis for an elaboration of the best and worst practices encountered in reference service.

Dramatic improvements in reference service could be achieved if reference librarians were trained to use the following five skills in every interview they conduct:

1. Use welcoming body language.

2. Ask open-ended questions.

3. Volunteer help.

4. Monitor the referral.

5. Use a follow-up question.

---

*From C. S. Ross and P. Dewdney, "Best Practices: An Analysis of the Best (and Worst) in Fifty-two Public Library Reference Transactions," *Public Libraries* 33 (1994): 261–266.

---

ticularly important. You should also present a separate oral report if you are recommending changes in reference policies and procedures in a specific organization.

Works Cited

Nassar, A. 1997. An evaluation of the Brandeis model of reference service at a small academic library. *Reference Librarian,* no. 58: 163–176.

Rose, P. M., K. Stoklosa, and S. A. Gray. 1998. A focus group approach to assessing technostress at the reference desk. *Reference & User Services Quarterly* 37: 311–317.

Ross, C. S., and P. Dewdney. 1994. Best practices: An analysis of the best (and worst) in fifty-two public library reference transactions. *Public Libraries* 33: 261–266.

Wei, W. 1995. Rethinking science library services: A user study at the University of California, Santa Cruz. *Science and Technology Libraries* 15: 17–42.

PART	REFERENCE ASSESSMENT
IV	**ANNOTATED BIBLIOGRAPHY**

This section contains a selective, annotated bibliography of key, accessible studies on the assessment of library reference services. We have tried to provide an overview of the variety of methods used to assess reference services over the years. In the annotations themselves, we have concentrated as much on the methods and techniques as on the findings and conclusions. Our working assumption has been that the readers of this book will be looking for practical advice on how to conceptualize, plan, implement, and evaluate a reference assessment project or program.

The annotated bibliography is sponsored and coordinated by the Evaluation of Reference and Adult Services Committee (ERASC), Management and Operation of User Services Section (MOUSS), Reference and User Services Association (RUSA), of the American Library Association. Some of the individual annotators (Paula Contreras, Patricia L. Gregory, A. Craig Hawbaker, Razia Nanji, Elaina Norlin, Eric Novotny, Mary Parker, Thomas A. Peters, and Jeanette Moore Piquet) are present or former members of the committee. The remaining annotators (Laura Dale Bischof, Jacob Carlson, Susan Clark, Frank Elliott, Lorrie Knight, John Mess, and Jim Stemper) are interested in the topic and have graciously written or revised annotations for the present chapter.

The asterisked entries have been newly annotated for this volume. Unasterisked entries are revised annotations from the *Reference Assess-*

ment Manual (Ann Arbor: Pierian, 1995), a publication project of the RUSA MOUSS Evaluation of Reference and Adult Services Committee. Sometimes the revisions have been minor, but at other times the "revision" has involved a complete reworking of the annotation. The goal of the *Reference Assessment Manual* was to highlight the "wide range of evaluation instruments useful in assessing reference service effectiveness," and "to encourage library administrators to support and promote evaluation of services." The intent of the present section is to provide librarians with a practical synopsis of the methods and findings of key reference assessment projects over the years. Generally, the primary sort for the entries is by chapter, and then alphabetically by the last name of the first author.

CHAPTER 1
PURPOSE OF THE EVALUATION

Economics of Reference Service

* Abels, Eileen G. 1997. Improving reference service cost studies. *Library and Information Science Research* 19: 135–152.

Most cost studies of reference service are based on the determination of an average unit cost of a particular service. These studies are beset by methodological problems, such as imprecise definition of services, variable units of work associated with the service costs, and a lack of reliability and validity in the measurement tools used to derive the costs. Typical transactions, such as mediated request services, end-user search services, and user education services, illustrate the problems associated with assigning average unit costs to the services. In addition, reference cost studies frequently fail to take into account shared or indirect costs. Resource allocation decisions are made arbitrarily for the purposes of the research. Abels suggests six strategies that would improve reference-service cost studies: the use of subcategories of service rather than single units; an increase in sample size; a broader interpretation of the organizational context; alternatives to arbitrary resource-allocation decisions; matching of the unit costs to the type of decision being made; and comparing cost to value. Each of these strategies offers opportunities for further research. (annotated by Lorrie Knight)

Henson, Jim. 1987. *Summary/analysis: Field responses to the reference referral study report*. Sacramento: California State Library.

Henson reports the results of a cost study of the California reference referral system, a service funded by the California Library Services Act. The study was initiated by the state librarian in anticipation of severe funding problems. The functions studied included question answering, statewide education and training, development of specialized resources, and quality control. A consultant examined the direct costs associated with handling questions, including staff time and benefits, database costs, telephone costs, materials purchased either for the center or for the host library, and supplies and equipment used in direct reference service. The costs of staff training and statewide educational functions were not included. The results indicated that the direct costs per reference question received ranged from $17 to $115, with an average of $31. The cost-saving recommendations made included consolidating the seventeen regional reference centers into a smaller number, instituting flexible guidelines to limit the amount of time spent on each question, using less-skilled personnel for routine searching, and increasing the question-handling productivity. (revised by Tom Peters)

Regazzi, John, and Rodney M. Hersberger. 1978. Queues and reference service: Some implications for staffing. *College & Research Libraries* 39: 293–298.

The authors studied instances of queuing at the reference desk at Northern Illinois University, a medium-sized academic library. Queuing theory and simulation technique were used to attempt to address this library management problem. The study explored alternative reference-desk staffing patterns for peak service periods. The data necessary to develop a simulation model were obtained by sampling patron arrival times and service time during periods of peak demand over six months. Based on the analysis, the authors concluded that a single-channel, two-stage reference service (i.e., where a librarian and a student assistant provide reference service in parallel, rather than in tandem) provided the highest cost-effectiveness rating, while minimizing queuing. (revised by Tom Peters)

Van House, Nancy A. 1983. A time allocation theory of public library use. *Library and Information Science Research* 5: 365–384.

Van House developed a conceptual model of public library use based on time allocation theory. The purpose of the study was to develop an economic model of the individual's decision to use the public library. A basic assumption behind this analysis is that, on average, people make decisions based on a rational assessment of their private costs and benefits. The model places library use in the context of a series of interrelated decisions made by the consumer about allocating time to various activities based on the relative costs and benefits. The cost of library use is a function of the amount of time required (which in turn depends on the library, the user, and the information need) and the cost per unit of time (which depends on the individual's wage rate). The cost of satisfying an information need depends on the user's wage rate, his or her ability to use the library, the purposes for which the information is sought, and library policies and procedures. Van House notes that the time allocation theory has implications for a library's effort to increase use among specific user groups, and it can inform discussions of possible user fees. (revised by Tom Peters)

See also the following annotation under chapter 4 of part IV: Harless and Allen (1999).

Quality of the Reference Service Process

* Bicknell, Tracy. 1994. Focusing on quality reference service. *Journal of Academic Librarianship* 20 (May): 77–81.

Bicknell exhorts readers to adopt a more customer-oriented service approach to reference. This requires reference staff to meet user needs rather than expecting users to adapt to their practices. The author identifies four aspects of quality, customer-oriented reference service: (1) user needs and expectations, (2) staff behaviors and communication skills, (3) the reference environment, and (4) staff morale and workload. The impact of each of these factors on reference service is discussed. Practical suggestions for evaluating and improving each aspect of reference service are provided. (annotated by Eric Novotny)

Dyson, Lillie Seward. 1992. Improving reference services: A Maryland training program brings positive results. *Public Libraries* 31: 284–289.

In this follow-up to the unobtrusive studies of reference service in public libraries done in 1983 and 1986, Dyson reports findings from a 1990–91 survey. Among the twenty-three Maryland library systems participating, the study found an overall decrease in the percentage of incorrect answers. This improvement is attributed to the use of the Model Reference Behaviors Checklist (reproduced in article), which was introduced after the 1983 survey. Librarians trained in the application of these behaviors performed significantly higher in this current study than those librarians without training. Furthermore, the highest-scoring library in this study used the checklist as a service requirement. A three-day model behaviors workshop followed by peer coaching and other activities is most associated with continued reference service improvement. Dyson concludes that communication behaviors are the determining variables in outstanding reference performance, and she notes that these behaviors can be learned. This study has obvious implications for all libraries that offer reference service. (revised by A. Craig Hawbaker)

Gers, Ralph, and Lillie J. Seward. 1988. "I heard you say" . . . peer coaching for more effective reference service. *Reference Librarian,* no. 22: 245–260.

Gers and Seward felt that their Better Communication Equals Better Reference Performance workshop was an effective learning experience that taught participants model behaviors leading to improved reference service. They were concerned, however, that the librarians would not use their new skills at work due to the extra effort, awkwardness, and greater discomfort associated with such an undertaking. In order to avoid this common pitfall, a peer coaching strategy combined with a reward system was also taught as a part of the workshop. Coaching is a mutual relationship in which two or more people agree to help each other use new skills and provide one another with feedback. Strategies to facilitate peer coaching are outlined. The dramatic success of peer coaching in two libraries over a three-year period is briefly summarized. (revised by A. Craig Hawbaker)

Jahoda, Gerald. 1989. Rules for performing steps in the reference process. *Reference Librarian,* nos. 25/26: 557–567.

Jahoda identifies and explores thirteen steps in the reference process, in terms of objectives and facts about each step, as well as rules for handling the facts. The thirteen steps are (1) message selection,

(2) should query be negotiated? (3) query negotiation, (4) is negotiated query answerable in the open literature? (5) should query be answered in library? (6) referral of query to other agency, (7) selection of types of answer-providing tools, (8) search sequence of types of answer-providing tools, (9) search online or printed tools? (10) selection of specific answer-providing titles, (11) selection of access points, (12) search and answer selection, and (13) answer negotiation. Jahoda states that rules about reference steps would be helpful when instructing future reference providers, when developing a framework for evaluating reference providers, and when planning to have certain steps performed by library clerks or computers. He assumes that reference librarians answer queries by matching the expressed need with their perceptions of potentially relevant portions of the bibliographic world. Jahoda concludes that six of the steps have the potential of being driven by rules stronger than rules of thumb. (revised by Tom Peters)

* Larson, Carole A., and Laura K. Dickson. 1994. Developing behavioral reference desk performance standards. *RQ* 33: 349–357.

The authors describe how the University of Nebraska at Omaha reference department devised standards for evaluating the performance of individual reference providers. The reference department consisted of both professional and paraprofessional staff, providing reference services for over 15,000 students, faculty, and staff. The article addresses issues faced in developing performance standards based on objective, easily observable criteria. A task force identified five major goals for achieving the department's service objectives: (1) acts in a manner that encourages patrons to ask questions; (2) conducts reference interview and follow-through; (3) knows and follows policies; (4) exhibits teamwork regarding working at the desk; and (5) exhibits knowledge of reference sources and continues to develop knowledge of collections and resources. For each goal, a set of definable, observable, desired behaviors was assigned. The list of behaviors for Goal 1 included, "Smiles when patron approaches desk" and "Establishes positive eye contact." The preliminary and final goals and associated behaviors are reproduced in three appendixes. The finalized standards have been incorporated into the reference department's training process for new employees, and are used by the department chair in conducting evaluations. The authors conclude that the adoption of these performance standards has promoted department team-work, improved desk performance, and raised morale. (annotated by Eric Novotny)

Layman, Mary, and Sharon Vandercook. 1990. Statewide reference improvement: Developing personnel and collections. *Wilson Library Bulletin* 64: 26–31.

> The authors describe the CORE Project (California Libraries for Reference Excellence), which sought to provide training and reference books to libraries in the state system without professionally staffed reference desks. A core set of reference works was identified by an expert panel, and these were provided to participating libraries. An initial four-hour training workshop was presented throughout the state and covered how to effectively use the identified basic reference tools and a model of reference behavior. During the second year of the grant, a "training corps" was organized and given training by Gers and Bolin. Additional workshops were provided to enhance reference skills for special user populations. In addition to workshops, self-paced materials and other instruction methods were made available. (revised by John Mess)

Nahl-Jakobovits, Diane, and Leon Jakobovits. 1988. Problem solving, creative librarianship and search behavior. *College & Research Libraries* 49: 400–408.

> The authors discuss problem solving in relation to search behavior and articulate a five-step model of the search process: clarify the question; identify a possible source for finding the information; translate the question into the words of the source; conduct the search; and locate the materials. They relate this process to bibliographic instruction, stressing the role of motivation in problem solving. They articulate nine groupings of skills involved in information processing and eight skills involved in note taking. They give a list of five common errors in copying call numbers, eight errors in using the catalog, and five errors in searching in general. They also analyze seven skills involved in solving research problems. Although the focus here is on end-user searching, many of the listed facets of information retrieval apply to the reference interaction as well. (revised by Tom Peters)

* Smith, Lisa L. 1991. Evaluating the reference interview: A theoretical discussion of the desirability and achievability of evaluation. *RQ* 31: 75–81.

> Smith argues that before we can begin to evaluate the reference interview, we must analyze and place it within its proper context in librarianship. She contends that most current research overstates the importance of the reference. A demystification of the process is seen as an integral part of adopting accurate and realistic standards for the reference interview. Several arguments are made supporting the view that the reference interview receives undue attention in the library literature. The author notes that the term is a relatively recent concept, not widely used prior to World War II. Several studies are cited which conclude that the reference interview is necessary for only a small fraction of questions posed by patrons. The reference interview is seen as only one element of library service, and not even the most important one. Only with the proper perspective can effective evaluation of the reference interview take place. The author concludes that such evaluation is necessary and desirable. While not necessarily the primary component of librarianship as a whole, the interview is a factor in library service, and therefore needs to be evaluated. Using a combination of evaluative techniques is advocated, including both unobtrusive and obtrusive observation, as well as qualitative and quantitative methods. If the available methodologies are used carefully, and within their limitations, effective evaluation is attainable. (annotated by Eric Novotny)

Stephens, Sandy, Ralph Gers, Lillie Seward, Nancy Bolin, and Jim Partridge. 1988. Reference breakthrough in Maryland. *Public Libraries* 27: 202–203.

> A 1983 research project that conducted unobtrusive studies of reference service in Maryland public libraries resulted in the usual 55 percent of reference questions that were answered completely and correctly. More importantly, researchers discovered twenty "model" communication behaviors that greatly improve reference performance. The three most important behaviors are: verifying or making sure that you hear the specific question being asked; asking a follow-up question; and using open-ended probing questions to draw out the patron's specific need. Believing that these model behaviors are within the control of the individual librarian, the authors designed a three-day workshop to teach the behaviors to

public library staff who answer reference questions. Next, a research firm conducted a second unobtrusive study comparing workshop-trained library staff with untrained staff. The results showed that trained staff answered more than 77 percent of the questions correctly, while untrained staff answered 60 percent correctly. This research suggests that training based on good research can yield results. (revised by A. Craig Hawbaker)

Taylor, Robert. 1968. Question-negotiation and information seeking in libraries. *College & Research Libraries* 29: 178–194.

Taylor presents an important detailed theoretical elaboration of the question negotiation process in libraries. A reference question is viewed as an often fuzzy description of an area of doubt which is dynamic, negotiable, and open-ended. Taylor divides the question formation process into four stages: the actual unexpressed need for information, the conscious description of need (still within the user's brain), the formal statement of the need, and the question presented to the information system within the constraints and grammar of that system. Librarians work with users as far back as the conscious description of need to clarify the meaning of questions and enable information systems to work most effectively. Librarians generally use five filters: determination of the subject, objective and motivation of the inquirer, personal characteristics of the inquirer, relationship of inquiry description to file organization, and anticipated or acceptable answers. Taylor emphasizes the dynamic nature of both the question process and the filtering mechanisms which need to be incorporated in an information system to give acceptable answers. Upon a conceptual basis of stages, filters, and their dynamic natures, Taylor presents a sound theoretical foundation for developing reference evaluation programs. He explores and explicates why libraries as communication channels are very frustrating and complex systems to use. Taylor notes that present systems are "object oriented (static) rather than inquiry oriented (dynamic)." (revised by Frank Elliott)

* Tyckoson, David A. 1992. Wrong questions, wrong answers: Behavioral vs. factual evaluation of reference service. *Reference Librarian,* no. 38: 151–173.

Tyckoson believes that evaluations of reference service based on librarians' answers to factual questions are simplistic measures of

a very complex process. While it is important for librarians to identify and use information sources effectively, this step in the reference
transaction plays a minor role in the overall process. Moreover,
user surveys in libraries of all types have found that a user's satisfaction is influenced more by the behavior of the librarian than
by the correctness of the librarian's answer. Tyckoson argues that
behavioral factors such as the librarian's willingness to make eye
contact, to listen, and to ask open-ended questions are important
variables of performance, and he calls for the profession to develop a set of guidelines for measuring the behavioral aspects of
reference service. Behavioral evaluation methods that could be
used in libraries include obtrusive evaluation by the supervisor;
obtrusive evaluation by peers; videotapes; and unobtrusive evaluation by patrons. (annotated by A. Craig Hawbaker)

See also the annotations in the following sections of part IV:

Chapter 4: Bostick (1993), Jardine (1995), King and Mahmoodi
(1991);

Chapter 5: Alafiatoayo, Yip, and Blunden-Ellis (1996), Dewdney
and Ross (1994), Durrance (1989), Durrance (1995), Gers and
Seward (1985), Ingwersen (1982), Ricks, Orth, and Buckley
(1991), Solomon (1997);

Chapter 6: Radford (1996), Radford (1999);

Chapter 7: Arthur (1990), Brown (1994), Devore-Chew, Roberts,
and Smith (1988), Gothberg (1976), Kuhlthau (1988),
Kuhlthau et al. (1990), Markham, Stirling, and Smith (1983),
Michell and Harris (1987), Radford (1998), Saracevic et al.
(1988), Von Seggern (1989).

Quality of Reference Service Resources

* Curry, Deborah A. 1992. Assessing and evaluating diversity in the
reference department. *Reference Librarian,* no. 38: 115–120.

Curry discusses the need to include diversity and multiculturalism
as criteria when evaluating reference staff and collections. The author notes that the many articles on reference assessment rarely
mention concepts related to diversity. She discusses the impor-

tance of recruitment and retention of non-white reference librarians, building reference collections to meet the needs of increasingly diverse student and faculty populations, and setting goals to increase diversity in reference departments. (annotated by Susan Clark)

Donnelly, Anna M. 1993. Reference environment problems checklist: A suggestion towards analyzing dysfunctional reference. In *First preconference on research in reference effectiveness,* ed. Marjorie Murfin and Jo Bell Whitlatch. RASD Occasional Paper 16. Chicago: American Library Association, Reference and Adult Services Division.

> Donnelly proposes a set of checklists to measure the environmental factors affecting reference service. She grouped the environmental factors into six areas: computers and equipment, the reference collection, the reference desk, staff training, the physical environment, and interunit cooperation. This list yielded eleven checklists with a total of 114 factors. The variables used to measure environmental factors included frequency of occurrence, impact on reference work, and handling (how well the reference staff dealt with the problem). Twenty libraries (fourteen academic libraries, five public libraries, and one special library) used the instrument to evaluate their own reference environment. The results showed a clear relationship among the three main variables— "usually, where one category (handling/frequency/impact) is poor or good, the other two follow suit." The results also show that a reference staff can perceive their environment in very different ways. An analysis of libraries that were also involved in the Wisconsin-Ohio Reference Evaluation Study showed that Donnelly's environmental factors checklist is best used with success-of-outcome measures "to obtain the most complete picture of areas needing improvement." The checklist instrument should work for any type of library because it is easy to administer, has sufficient detail, and offers an opportunity for reference staff to discuss the best ways to handle problems affecting their common work space. (revised by Jim Stemper)

* O'Connor, Daniel O., and Esther R. Dyer. 1990. Evaluation of corporate reference collections. *Reference Librarian,* no. 29: 21–31.

> The authors allude to the Penniman model for corporate libraries, which emphasizes access over ownership. Several research studies

indicate that corporate reference collections may differ from reference collections at other types of libraries. The authors question the applicability to corporate libraries of the assumptions commonly used to evaluate other reference collections: (1) the core reference collection is books, (2) reference collections are designed for repeat use, and (3) the "lock and key" model of reference service, where the reference collection is the lock and the reference query is the key. Before evaluating the reference collection of the corporate library at Empire Blue Cross and Blue Shield, the authors analyzed reference questions and found that executives had highly specialized information needs not addressed by the traditional reference collection, while staff had more traditional public-library types of questions. The authors concluded that the corporate library should disregard serving repeat users and provide priority service to senior management, thereby narrowing their service goal and concentrating efforts on collecting and designing services to ensure access to materials and information that support executive decision-making. A systematic review of the reference collection resulted in most items being discarded. The authors concluded that the two most important reference tools were the computer for online access and the telephone. (annotated by Susan Clark and Jeanette Moore Piquet)

* Richardson, John V., Jr. 1998. Question Master: An evaluation of a Web-based decision-support system for use in reference environments. *College & Research Libraries* 59: 29–37.

Question Master (QM) was designed to be an intelligent decision-support system (IDSS) that automates routine factual reference questions. QM is a series of HTML pages that guides a librarian through a set of clarifying questions before making a recommendation about the most appropriate electronic or print resource in OCLC's WorldCat catalog. An IDSS could free up reference librarians to answer more demanding questions, reduce reference service costs, and record the complete transaction for further analysis. Richardson conducted a usability study of QM's biographical module, containing 159 reference sources. Four librarians, selected by the OCLC Usability Lab, were asked to think aloud as they used QM, and their actions and verbalizations were videotaped. After the sessions, each participant completed a questionnaire and was interviewed by several people. The three goals of the research project were to support the decision-making process of reference librarians, to improve the accuracy of reference transactions, and to increase user satisfaction. The procedure for evaluating the accuracy of an expert system consisted of employing a set of validating, typical test questions, then scoring the answers on an eight-point scale, ranging from referral to a single source that provided a complete, correct answer, to referral to several sources, none of which provided an answer. Richardson found that the accuracy of QM was substantially better than most reported studies of real-world reference service. QM is available for public use and testing at http://purl.oclc.org/net/Question_Master. (annotated by Tom Peters)

Rinderknecht, Deborah. 1992. New norms for reference desk staffing adequacy: A comparative study. *College & Research Libraries* 53: 429–436.

Rinderknecht replicates the 1978–79 study published by Murfin in 1983 (*College & Research Libraries* 44: 321–333). Both studies used a method recommended by the Library Administration and Management Association's Task Force on Comparability of Reference Statistics. For this study, survey data were collected from 103 academic libraries during a typical week in the fall of 1988. Responding libraries were divided into five groups based on their weekly gate counts. Three of the five groups experienced an increase in the number of reference questions received during the sample week, with an overall average increase of 6 percent. In contrast, the overall average number of person-hours staffing the main reference desk decreased by 3 percent. Libraries with potential patron workloads (gate count divided by reference desk person-hours) exceeding two hundred have shown a tendency to fall short of a good level of reference success in the Wisconsin-Ohio Reference Evaluation Program. Rinderknecht notes that such norms are imperfect approximations, and thus do not provide absolute answers. Because they are drawn from existing conditions, norms should not be used as standards. Rinderknecht concludes that this type of assessment of reference staffing levels may help libraries to assess current and desired staffing levels; recognize potential deficiencies in providing public service by establishing a basis of comparison with similar institutions; and appraise the effects of change, especially the decline in real budgetary power. (revised by Tom Peters)

* Stalker, John C., and Marjorie E. Murfin. 1996. Why reference librarians won't disappear: A study of success in identifying answering sources for reference questions. *RQ* 35: 489–503.

> Undergraduate journalism students at Ohio State University participated in a study to determine if they could identify the correct sources to answer moderately difficult reference questions with the aid of an expert system database called SourceFinder (SOFI). Their performance was measured against a control group attempting the same task with the aid of the online catalog. Results showed that students searching the online catalog identified a correct answering source only 10.5 percent of the time, while those searching SOFI had a success rate of 58 percent, which increased to 78 percent after database modification. Based on these results, Stalker and Murfin conclude that searching for specific facts and information in reference sources through an academic library's online catalog is an almost impossible task with a very high expenditure of time for a very low rate of success. Their success rate with SOFI is encouraging, and they may work toward making it available on the Web, but only after needed enhancements and further assessment. (annotated by A. Craig Hawbaker)

* Su, Shiao-Feng, and F. W. Lancaster. 1995. Evaluation of expert systems in reference service applications. *RQ* 35: 219–228.

> The authors compared two expert systems: SourceFinder and Reference Expert. Both systems are designed to assist novice library users in their search for information sources on a topic. Beginning library school students at the University of Illinois at Urbana were given a predetermined set of questions. Half used SourceFinder and the other half used Reference Expert to identify resources. Their results were then compared with the resources recommended by librarians. Not surprisingly, the author determined that current expert systems are not yet able to match the performance of experienced reference librarians. In this study Reference Expert did a much better job of mimicking the advice given by librarians than did SourceFinder. Left unanswered by this article is whether either

resource would aid non-library school students in their research. (annotated by Eric Novotny)

* Tschanz, Virginia. 1991. Assessment of HyperCard program at Penrose Library, the University of Denver. *Reference Services Review: RSR* 19: 39–46.

> Computer-assisted reference services are a recent development. This article describes a HyperCard service implemented by the author. Penrose Tutorial and Guides is a computerized guide to the library's business information resources and the use of the online catalog and the CARL UnCover database. Students view a series of interconnected cards, beginning with a very general category, such as business information. They are guided through the stack of cards to more and more specific query terms. Ultimately, the student views a card that describes and locates a very specific resource. The specific titles included reflect the author's experience in constructing efficient business searches. Each student develops a personal information-retrieval path, aided by the navigational devices on each card. Students may also view a conceptual map that traces their search history or tutorial cards that explain the research process. Each type of card is illustrated in the article. The program offers built-in assessment devices, including a tool that records usage statistics for the menu cards and a suggestion box that allows users to submit feedback. The program is easy to use and very stable. User feedback is largely positive. The author concludes that the HyperCard-aided reference initiative is a service worthy of expansion. (annotated by Lorrie Knight)

See also the annotations in the following sections of part IV:

Chapter 4: Allen and Smith (1993), Ankeny (1991), Gunning and Spyers-Duran (1993), Lowenthal (1990), Nitecki (1993), Westbrook (1984), Willet (1992);

Chapter 5: Arrigona and Mathews (1988), Havener (1990), Havener (1993), Haynes et al. (1990), Hunter (1991), Peters (1989), Welch, Cauble, and Little (1997), Woodard (1989);

Chapter 6: Rose, Stoklosa, and Gray (1998);

Chapter 7: Puttapithakporn (1990).

ANNOTATED BIBLIOGRAPHY

Quality of Reference Service Products

* Chu, Felix T. 1996. Framing reference encounters. *RQ* 36: 93–101.

Organizational policies and procedures often affect the success of reference encounters. Chu examines the usefulness of four "frames" to describe the reference process: (1) the structural frame, which depends upon the boundaries of an organization; (2) the human resource frame, in which organizational success depends upon the self-actualization or need gratification of its employees; (3) the political frame, where the outcome of the event is determined by competition for scarce resources and the influence of conflicting power bases; and (4) the symbolic frame, which relies on the use of personal metaphors within organization cultures. A specific reference scenario is analyzed in the context of each frame, with varying degrees of success. Chu documents and discusses the existing literature that examines reference service using the four frames. Although every frame may not be applicable to every situation, this type of analysis is a useful way to examine a problem from a variety of perspectives. Reference librarians can employ these perspectives to develop satisfactory answers to patron inquiries. (annotated by Lorrie Knight)

Van House, Nancy A., Mary Jo Lynch, Charles R. McClure, Douglas L. Zweizig, and Eleanor Jo Rodger. 1987. *Output measures for public libraries: A manual of standardized procedures.* 2nd ed. Chicago: American Library Association.

Published just five years after the appearance of the first edition, this second edition incorporates various suggested refinements and improvements. More emphasis is placed on assessment activities that allow libraries serving similar communities and with similar resources to compare outputs and outcomes. The measurement methods have been made easier and more appropriate, explanations of terms and concepts have been expanded and clarified, more information is provided on how to interpret and apply the results, and measurement and evaluation activities are more closely integrated with library planning processes. Measurement tools and techniques for a variety of areas are provided, including reference services, materials use, library programming, and services for special populations. Instructions are provided on how to obtain the most valid, reliable, and comparable measures possible. (revised by Tom Peters)

Van House, Nancy A., Beth T. Weil, and Charles R. McClure. 1990. *Measuring academic library performance: A practical approach.* Chicago: American Library Association, Association of College and Research Libraries.

> The authors offer a variety of user-centered output measures for academic libraries. These output measures encompass various aspects of library collections and services, including circulation, materials availability, attendance, remote use, reference services, and others. The measures are intended to be replicable in all types of academic and research libraries, to be decision-oriented, to be easy and inexpensive to use, to be user-oriented, and to be tied to library goals and objectives. The measures were tested, refined, and retested at eleven academic libraries in California. The first part of the book covers measurement in general, output measures in particular, and their use for evaluation. The second part presents step-by-step guides to each measurement method. The authors provide practical advice on several data collection instruments for the assessment of reference service, including a seven-question reference satisfaction survey, a reference services statistics form, a service point data-collection form (i.e., a snapshot of the number of patrons using various service points in the library), and a six-question general satisfaction survey. The authors also provide practical advice on how to report the results of a survey. (revised by Tom Peters)

* Walter, Virginia A. 1995. Kids count: Using output measures to monitor children's use of reference services. *Reference Librarian,* nos. 49/50: 165–178.

> The main focus of this article is a discussion of how the creation of the first two documents, *Planning and Role Setting for Public Libraries (PRSPL)* and *Output Measures for Public Libraries (OMPL),* led to the creation of a third, *Output Measures for Public Library Service to Children (OMPLSC),* which could better address service to children and provide for the measurement of services to children. Of the eight roles outlined in *PRSPL,* the provision of reference

service is discussed in greatest depth. A good discussion is presented of its strengths and weaknesses in defining and measuring reference service, both to adults and to youth. (annotated by Jeanette Moore Piquet)

Weech, Terry L., and Herbert Goldhor. 1982. Obtrusive versus unobtrusive evaluation of reference service in five Illinois public libraries: A pilot study. *Library Quarterly* 52: 305–324.

The authors report on a pilot study to determine the relative effectiveness of obtrusive and unobtrusive methods of evaluating reference service. Staff in five public libraries were evaluated unobtrusively by using university students from the community as proxy reference patrons. The same library staff were then evaluated obtrusively by requesting them to provide the answers to a list of fifteen reference questions. Results showed a slight but statistically significant relationship existing between methods of evaluation and results of evaluation, indicating that library staff tend to answer a greater proportion of reference questions completely and correctly when they are aware of being evaluated. More studies are needed before definitive conclusions can be drawn. The article includes the question sets used in obtrusive study and the proxy evaluation form used in unobtrusive study. (revised by A. Craig Hawbaker)

See also the annotations in the following chapter of part IV:

Chapter 3: Saxton (1997), Tagliacozzo (1977), Van House (1985);

Chapter 4: Fairfax County Public Library (1988), Lowenthal (1990), Murfin and Bunge (1988a), Murfin and Gugelchuk (1987), Strong (1980), Whitlatch (1990a);

Chapter 5: Childers (1980), Elzy et al. (1991), Gers and Seward (1985), Halldorsson and Murfin (1977), Head and Marcella (1993), Hernon and McClure (1986a), Hernon and McClure (1986b), Hernon and McClure (1987), Isenstein (1991), Kantor (1981), King (1982), Paskoff (1991), Rodger and Goodwin (1987), Roy (1995), Van House and Childers (1984), Whittaker (1990), Woodard (1989);

Chapter 6: Childers (1997);

Chapter 7: Christensen et al. (1989).

CHAPTER 2
EVALUATION GOALS AND OBJECTIVES

* Latrobe, Kathy H., and W. Michael Havener. 1994. Addressing school library media reference services: Guidelines for success. *Reference Librarian,* no. 44: 161–172.

> Latrobe and Havener present an extensive building-level checklist (based on guidelines and standards from professional organizations) to be used to assess school-library media reference services. They discuss the value of using professional guidelines as a foundation for service assessment for all types of libraries, noting that such guidelines and the goals and standards they are based on are dynamic, and must change to reflect the times. Two specific documents served as the basis for this very thorough checklist: "Information Power: Guidelines for School Library Media Programs," written by the American Association of School Librarians and the Association for Educational Communications and Technology; and "Information Services for Information Consumers; Guidelines for Providers," written by the Standards and Guidelines Committee, Reference and Adult Services Division, American Library Association. "Information Power" stresses that the success of a school media center depends greatly on the integration of information services into the school curriculum in a way that fully supports the mission and goals of the organization, and on the full support of and leadership of the school's administration. "Information Services for Information Consumers" outlines goals for all types of libraries. Six major areas addressed by this document are services, resources, access, personnel, evaluation, and ethics. (annotated by Jeanette Moore Piquet)

* McCreight, Jo Ann O. 1992. Is the sky falling? Or using the policies and procedures manual as an evaluation tool. *Reference Librarian,* no. 38: 251–255.

> When the author's library underwent budget cuts, she found that it was crucial to have policies in place to evaluate collections and services. Her essay encourages librarians to maintain policies and procedures manuals in order to have benchmarks for evaluating and decision-making. When evaluating periodicals for cancellation, for example, it is important to have written objectives for collection development. Although evaluating reference services is not discussed in this essay, it is clear that written objectives and poli-

cies are important in evaluating all library services. (annotated by Susan Clark)

* Quinn, Brian. 1995. Improving the quality of telephone reference service. *Reference Services Review: RSR* 23 (4): 39–50.

Criteria are provided for evaluating quality telephone reference service: accuracy, speed, etiquette, versatility, and promotion. Establishing policy guidelines is important in defining quality service. Several studies of telephone reference are reviewed: most found an accuracy rate of about 50 to 60 percent. Issues of training and technology are discussed in detail. The author concludes that telephone reference service in general is neglected and underutilized. He advocates using the telephone as a powerful reference tool that will become more important as more students use remote access to databases and call from home with reference questions. (annotated by Susan Clark)

Suburban Library System Reference Service. 1988. *Reference evaluation manual for public libraries*. Oak Lawn, Ill.: Suburban Library System.

The five chapters in this manual address the five questions related to reference assessment that are of most interest to libraries in the Suburban Library System in Illinois: Are our patrons satisfied with the reference answers we provide? What subjects do people ask about most? What percentage of reference questions do we answer within one hour, 25 hours, 48 hours, or one week? How can the output measure "reference question per capita" (from the second edition of *Output Measures for Public Libraries*) be used as an evaluative measure? Are our patrons getting accurate and complete answers? The manual provides step-by-step instructions and reproducible forms for pursuing answers to these questions. The evaluation procedures were intended to be used at all reference points in the library, not just at the official reference desk. The main purpose of this manual is to give public librarians a means to measure the effectiveness of their reference services against their own standards for the role of reference in their libraries. (revised by Tom Peters)

Van House, Nancy A. 1986. Public library effectiveness: Theory, measures, and determinants. *Library and Information Science Research* 8: 261–283.

Van House places various efforts to determine the effectiveness of public libraries into a context of theoretical and empirical research on organizational effectiveness. The constructs, measures, and determinants of public library effectiveness are investigated. Van House shows how recent books on output measures and the planning process assume a goal-based definition of effectiveness. One possible model of the determinants of public library output measures is presented. Data from the Baltimore County Public Library System were used to evaluate the validity, reliability, and sensitivity of output measures. For four output measures, all within-library-branch correlations were strong and statistically significant at the .01 level. However, the reference fill-rate did not demonstrate reliability; within-branch correlation was not significantly different from zero. (revised by Tom Peters)

Zweizig, Douglas. 1984. Tailoring measures to fit your service: A guide for the managers of reference services. *Reference Librarian,* no. 11: 53–61.

Zweizig articulates the need to reduce time spent looking at meaningless data and to use data efficiently to improve reference performance. If data are to be useful to the library manager, they must relate to the planning of reference service. Because planning is done in a repeating series, measurement needs to be done periodically to inform the process. Because organizational goals change over time, measures must be adapted or replaced to remain relevant to the decision process. Guidance is provided regarding what should be measured and how the measure will work. Managers are urged to determine the degree of precision needed for each decision process and to sample for that level, and no more, because the purpose is to improve service, not to become bogged down in statistics. (revised by Tom Peters)

* Zweizig, Douglas, Debra Wilcox Johnson, Jane Robbins, and Michele Besant. 1996. *The Tell it! manual: The complete program for evaluating library performance.* Chicago: American Library Association.

This resource provides an overview of the evaluative process in very accessible language and format. An emphasis is on the often neglected early stages of the research process. Readers are exhorted to develop a vision for the library and to keep this vision in mind as they conduct their research. The work is intended to be generally applicable, and as such it focuses on broad topics and guidelines. While the book is useful in any library setting, sections on special topics such as evaluating bookmobile usage, or interviewing young children, make this an especially valuable resource for public librarians. A useful feature is the inclusion of numerous sample exercises, tip sheets, forms, and checklists at the ends of chapters. (annotated by Eric Novotny)

See also the following annotation in the chapter 4 section of part IV: Van House and Childers (1993).

CHAPTER 3
CHARACTERISTICS OF GOOD MEASURES

Baker, Sharon L., and F. Wilfrid Lancaster. 1991. *The measurement and evaluation of library services*. 2nd ed. Arlington, Va.: Information Resources Pr.

This work summarizes and evaluates research findings and trends for all types of library services, with an emphasis on public services broadly defined. The authors synthesize the major discoveries, providing guidance to librarians unfamiliar with conducting research. Information is provided for evaluating services such as reference collections, online catalogs, database searching, and question answering. For each topic the major methodologies are described, with a discussion of their strengths and weaknesses. All library types are included; numerous findings and studies conducted in public libraries are described. Chapter 5 on "In-House Use" presents useful information on gathering data on library materials that do not circulate. Another especially useful section is chapter 10, which provides an overview of the emerging field of library standards. (revised by Eric Novotny)

* Busha, Charles H., and Stephen P. Harter. 1980. *Research methods in librarianship: Techniques and interpretation*. New York: Academic Pr.

Those attracted to the science part of library and information science will be most interested in this work. The authors advocate the adoption of the scientific method by library researchers. Not surprisingly given this perspective, a significant portion of the book is devoted to statistical analysis and techniques. The authors discuss in detail concepts such as variability, normal distribution, correlation, and statistical significance. In the sections on research methods, numerous examples of prior research are presented. These provide real-world examples of research studies conducted using the methodology being discussed. Although somewhat dated (the chapter on electronic calculators is an example), this work provides a useful, comprehensible overview of research, aimed specifically at librarians. (annotated by Eric Novotny)

Childers, Thomas. 1987. The quality of reference: Still moot after twenty years. *Journal of Academic Librarianship* 13: 73–74.

> Childers, who along with Crowley introduced the unobtrusive research method to librarianship, observes that after twenty years studies using the method continue to conceive the reference process and to use the unobtrusive method in roughly the same way it was in the first two studies reported. Childers argues that this unrealistically limits the idea of reference, given the range and variety of reference services commonly offered. Without systematic investigation, we cannot assert that the correctness of responses to factual questions is a key indicator of the overall quality of a library's reference service. No reported empirical data link performance on one kind of reference service with performance on another type of service. (revised by Tom Peters)

Cronbach, Lee J. 1950. Further evidence on response sets and test design. *Educational and Psychological Measurement* 10: 3–31.

> Cronbach notes that continuum scales (e.g., least-greatest, agree-disagree) are prone to a condition known as response sets—the tendency of a rater to mark most or all responses in a particular way. Response sets tend to dilute a test and lower its value. This condition frequently manifests itself in library surveys in the form of a strong positive bias. For example, instead of giving serious and thoughtful consideration to his or her own perceptions in regard to each question on a survey, the respondent simply finishes the rating task quickly by marking all boxes in the two most-favored categories. This tendency appears to be triggered by unanchored scales, where the meaning of the five points between the top and bottom are not clearly defined. In situations where raters are uncertain which of two ratings to give, they tend to assign the higher rating. As a consequence, most ratings on library surveys with unanchored continuum scales are likely to be inflated somewhat. Cronbach recommends "best choice" answers be used instead.

Possible answer choices are given in descriptive phrases, as in a multiple-choice test. He notes in regard to unanchored items that "any form of measurement where the subject is allowed to define the situation for himself in any way is to be avoided." (revised by Paula Contreras)

Emerson, Katherine. 1977. National reporting on reference transactions, 1976–1978. *RQ* 16: 199–207.

Emerson reviews the history of the development of definitions for reference and directional transactions. A reference transaction is defined as an information contact that involves the use, recommendation, interpretation, or instruction in the use of one or more information sources, or knowledge of such sources, by a member of the reference/information staff. Information sources include print and nonprint materials; machine-readable databases (including computer-assisted instruction); library bibliographic records, excluding circulation records; other libraries and institutions; and persons both inside and outside the library. A question answered through utilization of information gained from previous consultation of such sources is considered a reference transaction, even if the source is not consulted again. A directional transaction is an information contact that facilitates the use of the library in which the contact occurs and its environs, and that may involve the use of sources describing the library, such as schedules, floor plans, handbooks, and policy statements. Examples of directional transactions are directions for locating facilities such as rest rooms, carrels, and telephones; directions for locating library staff and users; directions for locating materials for which the user has a call number; supplying materials such as paper and pencils; and assisting users with the operation of machines. (revised by Paula Contreras)

* Evaluation of Reference and Adult Services Committee. Reference and Adult Services Division. American Library Association. 1995. *Reference assessment manual.* Ann Arbor: Pierian.

This wide-ranging resource serves two functions. The first half of the book contains literature reviews of the major themes in reference assessment. These include topics such as assessing staff morale, collection use, reference accuracy, staff training, and service outcomes. Each chapter discusses the scope of the field, the current state of research, and future research needs. The chapters are written by authorities such as Marjorie Murfin and Jo Bell Whitlatch. The latter half of the book provides an extensively annotated bibliography, along with reviews of assessment instruments (surveys, tests, studies, etc.). Information is provided about the function, reliability, and availability of many of the measures that have been designed to assess reference services. A nice feature of this book is that users can elect to purchase a supplementary disk containing the text of many of the test instruments themselves. Purchasers of both resources can go directly from the review to the test instrument on disk. (annotated by Eric Novotny)

* Hernon, Peter, and Ellen Altman. 1998. *Assessing service quality: Satisfying the expectations of library customers*. Chicago: American Library Association.

Hernon and Altman want to put customers at the center of the process of evaluating library services. The service quality movement views the service provided by an organization from the perspective of the customer. The authors provide in-depth examinations (with numerous examples) of data collection methods and measurement strategies for measuring service quality in public and academic libraries. Both quantitative and qualitative methods are covered. Entire chapters are devoted to surveys and focus group interviews. They argue that the touchstones of a viable library are customers, satisfaction, loyalty, and reputation. The authors distinguish between service quality and customer satisfaction. Service quality encompasses the interactive relationship between a library and the population it is supposed to serve. A customer is the recipient of any product or service provided by the organization. They argue that the library profession needs to focus on more meaningful indicators of customer loyalty, expectations, preferences, and satisfaction. Their intention with this book is to present some new ways to think about service, along with some methods for evaluating and improving service. (annotated by Tom Peters)

* Hults, Patricia. 1992. Reference evaluation: An overview. *Reference Librarian,* no. 38: 141–149.

Hults provides an overview of the literature of reference assessment and offers comparisons of various methods. Interestingly, the evaluation of reference service does not have extended historical roots. Fewer than forty articles on the subject were published prior to the late 1960s. Many of the early studies dealt with the quantitative results of data gathering. When patron surveys were employed, they often focused on patron satisfaction with the service, rather than on the accuracy of the responses. The decade of the 1970s marked the use of unobtrusive testing to assess reference quality. Librarians questioned the accuracy of such testing, as well as the design and application of the tests. Based on this examination of the literature, Hults offers recommendations for successful assessment programs. Librarians who wish to measure reference service quality must develop clear goals for the study, determine what information is needed, and identify appropriate measurement and data analysis tools. Response to the assessment is an essential follow-up step. Assessment programs that lead to improved reference services are important activities for librarians. (annotated by Lorrie Knight)

Kesselman, Martin, and Sarah Barbara Watstein. 1987. The measurement of reference and information services. *Journal of Academic Librarianship* 13: 24–30.

The authors reviewed literature about the use of statistics to measure reference and resources use for the 1960s, 1970s, and 1980s. Little was published about the topic before the 1970s, and much of it was negative in regard to the time spent collecting such data and the worthiness of the endeavor. The literature of the 1970s reveals a growing awareness of the need to gather data, and shows reference statistics becoming a field of study in and of itself. By the 1980s the gathering and analysis of statistics was viewed as a valuable tool for the management of libraries. The authors' study tested how consistent reference-desk personnel were in classifying reference queries. Different staff members classified the same question differently as short reference, long reference, directional, or referral. Most of the inconsistencies arose from differing conceptions of directional versus referral information, short versus long reference, and reference versus directional questions. (revised by Laura Dale Bischof)

* Murfin, Marjorie E. 1995. Evaluation of reference service by user report of success. *Reference Librarian,* nos. 49/50: 229–241.

The history of reference assessment methods includes user reports, librarian self-reports, behavioral guidelines, and unobtrusive testing. Murfin describes each method, reports the significant literature about it, and comments on its strengths and shortcomings. User reporting is determined to be an essential component of successful reference-service evaluation. It is representative of the actual process, accounts for environmental variables, and is desirable, useful information for librarians. Murfin discusses many of the problems inherent in user-report surveys and suggests strategies to overcome them. The criteria for the design of an assessment instrument include reliability and validity, the ability to account for multiple factors and environmental variables, incorporation of patron and librarian feedback devices, provision for data comparability, provision for interpretability, separation of user success and user satisfaction, control for positive bias in scale design, and control for positive bias in survey administration. Specific existing instruments are noted and compared. While no single methodology can provide a complete explanation of reference success, librarians cannot discount the importance of user input into the evaluation process. (annotated by Lorrie Knight)

Sandore, Beth. 1990. Online searching: What measure satisfaction? *Library and Information Science Research* 12: 33–54.

Sandore used quantitative measures to examine potential indicators of user satisfaction with a mediated online search service. A telephone survey of approximately 200 users of the Computer-Assisted Reference Center (CARC) of the Chicago Public Library was conducted over a five-month period. Based on a random sampling, each client was phoned approximately two weeks after the online search had been performed, and asked to complete a phone survey concerning their experiences with the search and the search results. The participation rate was 85 percent, yielding 171 completed surveys. The survey focused on what users had done with the information they received, their satisfaction with the information, how often they used the mediated online search service, and its usefulness to them. Survey data were validated and supplemented by data sheets completed by CARC staff at the time the users requested searches. General satisfaction was 91 percent, but specific satisfaction with the search results was 60 percent. Only 53 percent of the clients who were present during the search were satisfied, compared to 73 percent of those not present. The results indicated a low overall association between precision and satisfaction, regardless of whether the users' expectations were for exhaustive (high-recall) or specific (high-precision) results. Forty-one percent of the respondents attempted to locate and read only five to nine of the citations retrieved via the online search. (revised by Tom Peters)

* Saxton, Matthew L. 1997. Reference service evaluation and meta-analysis: Findings and methodological issues. *Library Quarterly* 67: 267–289.

Meta-analysis is a group of techniques that enables the analyzer to draw conclusions based on the findings of previous studies. Saxton asks several meta-analysis questions about the numerous studies since 1965 that have attempted to evaluate the quality of reference service: How often have the same variables been examined across different studies? To what extent do the observed correlations agree or disagree? Can the results from numerous studies be combined to obtain a more accurate estimate of the strength of association between a given variable and accurate reference service? Saxton found that five independent variables—library expenditures, number of volumes added, fluctuations in the collection, size of the service population, and hours of service—consistently exhibit across studies a moderate positive association with accurate reference service. Saxton notes, however, that quality and consistency in the reporting of findings have considerable impact on the success and validity of the meta-analysis. He concludes that, while meta-analysis can be applied to synthesizing research concerning reference service assessment, at present the technique is not highly effective because the data are sparse, fragmentary, and heterogeneous. (annotated by Tom Peters)

Tagliacozzo, Renata. 1977. Estimating the satisfaction of information users. *Bulletin of the Medical Library Association* 65: 243–249.

Tagliacozzo analyzed data from a study where a follow-up questionnaire was sent to a sample of MEDLINE users who had requested searches at seven information centers within a two-month period. Ninety percent of the respondents found the searches to have some degree of helpfulness, 80 percent found them generally to have some usefulness, while the percentage who found some relevant references was closer to 60 percent. Users who had the most knowledge of the subject (and who found missed references) rated the service lower than those with the least knowledge (who found no missed references). Tagliacozzo recommends that a single overall judgment of a service should be examined with suspicion, in particular if the rating scale measures a global judgment of the service (e.g., helpfulness, success, worthiness, or value), rather than an appraisal of specific search results. A questionnaire survey therefore should not be limited to eliciting an overall judgment, but should explore several aspects of the user's reaction to the outcome of his or her request for information. (revised by Tom Peters)

Van House, Nancy A. 1985. Output measures: Some lessons from Baltimore County Public Library. *Public Libraries* 24: 102–105.

Output measures are valuable tools to determine the effectiveness of library services. The Baltimore County Public Library selected several measures from *Output Measures for Public Libraries* to use in a multiyear study. Six measures were selected, data were collected, and the results were analyzed by branch and across the system. The author describes the use and interpretation of the measures and critiques their validity and applicability for use in other libraries. Certain inherent problems in data collection, sampling, and variable user populations are discussed. Van House concludes that although they are not perfect, output measures provide library managers with useful information for service assessment. (revised by Lorrie Knight)

* Westbrook, Lynn. 1989. *Qualitative evaluation methods for reference services: An introductory manual.* Washington, D.C.: Office of Management Services, Association of Research Libraries.

Westbrook presents a primer on qualitative evaluation methods. She defines qualitative evaluation (i.e., the examination and analysis of individual experiences) within the context of the usefulness of these methods for library management and staff. Westbrook argues that qualitative evaluation can help plan for and improve reference services. An evaluation program is a cyclical growth process, rather than an end in itself. Methods range from open-ended survey questions to in-depth interviews to ethnographic study techniques refined by anthropologists. Four specific techniques are presented from a practical point of view: observation, interviews, surveys, and content analysis (i.e., the examination of the written products of a specific task or process to find patterns and insights). For each technique, Westbrook presents guidelines in terms of the need for time, funding, and other resources. Triangulation, perhaps the most important principle of qualitative research, is the process by which a combination of methods is used to explore a single situation. Westbrook assumes that readers have a rudimentary knowledge of sampling methods, questionnaire design, interviewing skills, data analysis, and the basic ethical concerns about the treatment of human subjects. This is a practical, straightforward, well-organized manual. (annotated by Elaina Norlin)

* Westbrook, Lynn. 1990. Evaluating reference: An introductory overview of qualitative methods. *Reference Services Review: RSR* 18: 73–78.

Westbrook focuses on providing a general overview for those conducting their first qualitative assessments. Emphasis is placed on background information and definitions. Qualitative evaluation is defined as being concerned with the question of why, rather than how much. Different forms of qualitative research are discussed, including observation, group interviews, and open-ended surveys. The advantages and disadvantages of each form of research are outlined, and the author provides some examples of when and how each is best used. The article includes suggestions for planning a qualitative project and a selected list of resources for further reading. (annotated by Eric Novotny)

* White, Marilyn Domas, and Eileen G. Abels. 1995. Measuring service quality in special libraries: Lessons from service marketing. *Special Libraries* 86: 36–45.

As part of a Special Library Association project, the authors survey the literature of marketing to determine the applicability of service assessment models and instruments (e.g., SERVQUAL and SERV-PERF) to library services. Services, especially information services, are often more difficult to assess for quality than are goods. The quality of reference services, for example, may be judged on both the quality of the information and the quality of the service itself. In addition, reference quality assessment may be related to long-term, rather than single transaction, factors. White and Abels compare two instruments widely used as measures of client satisfaction. SERVQUAL measures service quality by comparing customer expectations and service performance. SERVPERF is based on performance evaluation only. Both instruments have advantages and disadvantages for use in special libraries. While SERVQUAL is more complex to administer, it has been rigorously tested and is content rich. SERVPERF is shorter and easier to administer and may be a more accurate predictor of behavioral variance. More studies are needed that test the applicability of these instruments to library service assessment. (annotated by Lorrie Knight)

Whitlatch, Jo Bell. 1989. Unobtrusive studies and the quality of academic reference services. *College & Research Libraries* 50: 181–194.

Whitlatch notes that Hernon and McClure and others who have undertaken unobtrusive assessment of reference service in academic libraries have used factual queries. Whitlatch suggests that factual queries are a minority of all queries and thus do not adequately represent the main body of questions handled by an academic reference staff. By using matching questionnaires for users and librarians, the author conducted a study of 397 reference transactions in five academic libraries in northern California. Sixty-six percent of users reported finding what was wanted, and 75 percent reported being satisfied. Whitlatch also collected data on questions asked and answers supplied and then classified the questions into three categories: factual, bibliographic (i.e., specific title), and subject/instrumental. Of the total, 11.3 percent were for specific facts, 18 percent were for location of specific citations, and 70.7 percent were subject or source related. Whitlatch found that users reported significantly different success rates for each question category. She also reports that librarians tend to judge factual questions to be more difficult because answering factual questions involves the use of less familiar, less frequently used sources. (revised by Tom Peters)

* Whitlatch, Jo Bell. 1992. Reference services: Research methodologies for assessment and accountability. *Reference Librarian,* no. 38: 9–19.

Whitlatch presents a review of research methods for the development and effective deployment of reference assessment programs. The author analyzes quantitative and qualitative assessment methodologies, describes the environment in which such assessment can be successful, and introduces several data-gathering strategies. Effective assessment programs begin with careful definition of goals and evaluation standards. Data collection methods should be appropriate to fulfilling these goals. Measurement devices should be reliable, valid, and replicable. Whitlatch examines quantitative studies, surveys, observation, and case studies as data collection methodologies. She explains each method and discusses its strengths and weaknesses for library applications. Whitlatch proposes a four-step plan for the design and implementation of an effective study. Although reference service evaluation is not an easy undertaking, ongoing studies by librarians will offer insights into the most effective ways of testing, understanding, and improving the reference process. (annotated by Lorrie Knight)

See also the annotations in the following sections of part IV:

Chapter 1—Quality of Reference Service Products: Van House et al. (1987), Walter (1995), Weech and Goldhor (1982);

Chapter 4: D'Elia and Walsh (1983);

Chapter 5: Hernon and McClure (1987), King (1982), Whittaker (1990).

CHAPTER 4
SURVEYS AND QUESTIONNAIRES

* Adams, Mignon S., and Jeffrey A. Beck, comps. 1995. *User surveys in college libraries*. CLIP Notes 23. Chicago: American Library Association.

This CLIP Note contains a variety of survey instruments previously used by college libraries. Samples of other related materials, such as cover letters, interview scripts, and final reports, are also included. The introduction provides an overview of a survey conducted of college librarians detailing general practices and feelings about survey research. (annotated by Eric Novotny)

* Allen, Frank R., and Rita Hoyt Smith. 1993. A survey of telephone inquiries: Case study and operational impact in an academic library reference department. *RQ* 32: 382–391.

In the early 1990s the Reference and Information Services Department of the John C. Hodges Library, University of Tennessee at Knoxville, faced declining budgets and a mandate to modify or reduce existing programs and services. Additionally, the staff perceived a decline in reference service due to constant telephone interruptions. A survey of telephone queries was designed and administered to examine the efficiency and effectiveness of the library's telephone reference service. The main goals of the survey were: (1) to determine the nature of calls received via the telephone, and (2) to determine the extent to which the current service could be streamlined. The survey was conducted over two separate one-week periods, during which all incoming calls were recorded. Calls were categorized by question type, time of day, approximate answer time, and whether assistance was needed in answering the caller's question. The results indicated that only 33.5 percent of calls received were categorized as reference by the person answering the call. The authors also used a process called queuing theory to analyze how many phone lines were needed to effectively handle reference traffic. The authors concluded that nonprofessionals could effectively handle much of the large volume of telephone questions received. Specific recommendations for modifying telephone reference service are provided. (annotated by Eric Novotny)

Ankeny, Melvon L. 1991. Evaluating end-user services: Success or satisfaction? *Journal of Academic Librarianship* 16: 352–356.

Ankeny examined user perceptions of end-user searching of business databases. In a preliminary study, 81.5 percent of the untrained end-users rated online business services highly, and 77.9 percent felt they obtained their information successfully. The author expressed concern that success and satisfaction were overrated. A second study was launched using the Wisconsin-Ohio Reference Evaluation Program. A successful search was defined as meeting all three criteria: (1) users found exactly what they were looking for, (2) were fully satisfied with the search, and (3) none of ten listed reasons for disappointment were selected. Of 600 questionnaires, 233 responses (38.8 percent) were categorized as successful. Of the 257 which listed causes of dissatisfaction, they reported system problems (18.7 percent), inappropriate topic (3.9 percent), and other (77.4 percent)—such as amount of information, relevancy, or content level of the retrieved information. The author concludes users do not have high success rates, and that satisfaction does not adequately measure success. Despite some design problems, the study raises interesting questions about online business tools, points to problems in other online systems, and makes the issue of measuring searching success a useful tool for service improvement. (revised by John Mess)

* Association of Research Libraries. Systems and Procedures Exchange Center. 1994. *User surveys.* SPEC Kit 205. Washington, D.C.: Association of Research Libraries.

> This SPEC Kit contains the results of a 1994 survey on the use of surveys by 69 ARL libraries. Sample surveys are provided by numerous academic institutions. Various survey formats are included. Earlier SPEC Kits dealing with surveys and user studies are *User Surveys and Evaluation of Library Services* (no. 71, 1981), *User Studies in ARL Libraries* (no. 101, 1984), and *User Surveys* (no. 148, 1988). (annotated by Eric Novotny)

Bostick, Sharon. 1993. The development and validation of the library anxiety scale. In *First preconference on research in reference effectiveness,* ed. Marjorie Murfin and Jo Bell Whitlatch. RASD Occasional Paper 16. Chicago: American Library Association, Reference and Adult Services Division.

> Bostick explains the development, distribution, and analysis of a reliable and valid survey instrument to measure library anxiety, especially for college and university students. Bostick discusses the process of seeking advice and the successive steps necessary for reducing the number of potential survey questions from 294 to 43. The primary tool used in question reduction was factor analysis, a technique often used in social sciences research for exploring the structure in a data set. Factor analysis helps to reveal those questions which explain the most variance in a data set. The final survey instrument of 43 questions explained 51.8 percent of the total variance in library anxiety. Factor analysis also allows a researcher to see how the variables group together into categories called factors. For example, the final survey instrument indicated that there were five primary factors in explaining library anxiety: barriers with staff, affective barriers, comfort with the library, knowledge of the library, and mechanical barriers. Barriers with staff was by far the most important, explaining 25.4 percent of the variance. Another interesting finding of this study was that students of all types over age 50 reported more library anxiety than younger students. This article highlights the importance of a class of statistical

tools often called data reduction tools: factor analysis, cluster analysis, and multidimensional scaling. (revised by Frank Elliott)

Budd, John, and Mike DiCarlo. 1982. Measures of user evaluation at two academic libraries: Prolegomena. *Library Research* 4: 71–84.

> The libraries of Northeast Louisiana University and Southeast Louisiana University collaborated to obtain quantitative measures of users' assessment of reference services. The authors adapted the assessment instrument developed by Steven Chwe (*California Librarian* 39: 46–55), which had been designed primarily for public libraries. The results of the surveys were used at both universities for broader institutional self-study and evaluation. Separate questionnaires were constructed for faculty and students. A six-point scale was used for respondents to rate both the importance of specific library services and library performance in these service areas. The basic inference drawn from this study was that faculty members from both universities perceived deficiencies in library services. They were, however, more satisfied with the services than with the collections. For the student survey, the questionnaires were mailed to one thousand students selected at random, with return postage included as an effort to elicit responses from non-users. The student responses, in contrast to the faculty responses, rated librarian performance on services lower than collection and environmental conditions. Students evidently believed that librarians are not sufficiently willing to help students, nor do they spend enough time on student reference questions. Students also were dissatisfied with the answers provided by librarians. (revised by Tom Peters)

* Childers, Thomas, Cynthia Lopata, and Brian Stafford. 1991. Measuring the difficulty of reference questions. *RQ* 31: 237–243.

> The authors report on a project to develop a measure of the difficulty of reference questions. They maintain that without differentiating between easy and difficult questions, reference evaluation studies may obtain inaccurate or misleading results. The authors review previous attempts to measure question difficulty, including type of question, length of question, type of source consulted, time required to answer, anticipated effort, and answering success. Questions handled by the California interlibrary reference referral network form the basis of this study. Data were collected on 658

questions received during 1990. Two survey forms were designed for each question submitted to the system. These measured nine factors, including Predicted Difficulty (measured by the librarian prior to attempting a response), Actual Difficulty (judged by the respondent after answering), Prior Knowledge of Subject, Time Spent in Answering, and Number of Sources Consulted. A high correlation was found between Predicted Difficulty and Actual Difficulty. The authors conclude that measuring Actual Difficulty is the preferred evaluative method. The observed high correlation between Predicted Difficulty and Actual Difficulty, however, allows libraries to make use of the former measure if the latter is more difficult to obtain. Similarly, Time Spent in Answering could serve as a reasonable approximation for Actual Difficulty due to the strong correlation between the two. The article includes examples of the survey forms. (annotated by Eric Novotny and Paula Contreras)

Childers, Thomas, and Nancy A. Van House. 1989. The grail of goodness: The effective public library. *Library Journal* 114: 44–49.

The emphasis in research about the effectiveness of public libraries has been in measuring outputs, such as the number of clients served or the amount of material circulated. The authors draw on research and theories from the field of management that present effectiveness in a cluster of models, including an output or goal model, a process model, a resource model, and a multiple constituencies model. The aim of this study was to better define library effectiveness as a multileveled concept. The authors focus on the multiple constituencies model, whereby library success is defined and perceived differently by different client groups, such as library employees and managers, trustees, friends, patrons, and community leaders. The authors devised a survey tool in which over 2,000 participants from different constituent groups ranked 257 indicators of library effectiveness. These indicators were identified through interviews with members from the various peer groups. The study revealed similarities across the constituent groups. The indicators were grouped into eight major dimensions of effectiveness that reflect the different models of organizational effectiveness prominent in the management literature. Academic libraries might also be well served by this type of multiple-constituent satisfaction survey. (revised by Laura Dale Bischof)

Clark, Philip M., and James Benson. 1985. Linkages between library uses through the study of individual patron behavior. *RQ* 24: 417–426.

> The authors note that the reference question often serves as the basic unit of measurement and analysis for reference assessment. They wanted to study the relationship between the asking of reference questions and other uses of library collections and services by individual users. They suggest that the individual user should be used as the basic unit of measurement. In this sense, the research reported here is user-centered. They note that not all reference questions and directional questions are asked at the reference desk. For this study, Clark and Benson examined the co-occurrence of borrowing and question-asking behavior, with gender and duration of visit as the two independent variables. In an attempt to collect data that were not subject to respondent error, data about patron behaviors were recorded onto a questionnaire form by library staff members, not by the patrons themselves. The patrons carried the questionnaire with them throughout the duration of their visit to the library. The study was conducted in February 1981 in the main library and two branches of the Sussex County Library System in New Jersey. The authors concluded that circulation and reference counts measured only part of the total outputs of public libraries. (revised by Tom Peters)

* Crawford, Gregory A. 1994. A conjoint analysis of reference services in academic libraries. *College & Research Libraries* 55: 257–267.

> Patrons are not monolithic in their desire for reference services. What is important to some may not be important to others. When measuring the value of services, we need to take into account this difference in values. To address this situation, Crawford used an evaluative technique known as conjoint, or trade-off, analysis. It has been used as a tool for market research to determine consumer preferences. The approach assumes that individual behaviors are based on choices among competing interests. Users are asked to assign higher values to the services they prefer. Libraries that receive higher scores on this type of analysis are offering services their patrons value more, and therefore can be said to be doing a better job of meeting patron preferences. The author discusses the results of a conjoint analysis undertaken by three academic institutions: Rutgers University, Moravian College, and Warren County Community College. A total of six attributes were included in the

study with trade-off matrices: (1) definitiveness (i.e., the likelihood that an answer to a question can be found in materials given to a patron by a librarian), (2) hours of service, (3) cost of service, (4) in-line wait time, (5) number of items retrieved to answer a question, and (6) service time. The study was based on a previous study by Halperin and Starzdon (see below). (annotated by Eric Novotny and Razia Nanji)

* Dalton, Gwenda M. E. 1995. Quantitative approach to user satisfaction in reference service evaluation. *South African Journal of Library and Information Science* 60: 89–103.

Dalton developed and tested a quantitative user-satisfaction assessment instrument at Unisa Library, University of South Africa. The "disconfirmation of expectation" method from the field of marketing, which is used to measure and evaluate an individual's responsive feelings toward a service, served as the basis for the instrument, with satisfaction defined as "the difference between the average actual performance of the service provided and the average expectations of the users." Analysis was limited to service provided by subject reference librarians to master's and doctoral degree students who were registered up to June 30, 1989. Questionnaires with 25 questions were mailed to 500 students in February 1990 asking for return three weeks later. Results were received for 367 completed questionnaires (73.4 percent), but after examining the responses, a proposal was made to shorten the questionnaire to 18 questions. Dalton discusses methods of measuring the reliability of the instrument (using Cronbach's alpha coefficient) and the validity of the user satisfaction construct. This quantitative method and survey proved valid for evaluating user satisfaction and could be adapted for wider application in other areas of libraries or in different library settings and with more varied clientele. (annotated by Patricia L. Gregory)

* Davis, Deborah S., and Alan M. Bernstein. 1997. From survey to service: Using patron input to improve customer satisfaction. *Technical Services Quarterly* 14 (3): 47–62.

When the American Library Association asked libraries to administer a customer satisfaction survey during the 1994 National Library Week, Odum Library at Valdosta State University in Georgia participated to gain insights into customers' attitudes and needs, as well as to compare local services with other academic libraries nationwide. Davis and Bernstein concluded that the unstructured comments provided by student respondents were much more valuable than their answers to the structured questions, where the response choices were a five-point Likert-type scale. (annotated by Tom Peters and Jeanette Moore Piquet)

D'Elia, George, and Sandra Walsh. 1983. User satisfaction with library service—a measure of public library performance? *Library Quarterly* 53: 109–133.

> The authors question whether user satisfaction is a valid measure of library performance. By means of an in-house, self-administered questionnaire, 623 public library patrons were asked questions designed to provide both a direct and indirect measure of their satisfaction. Data were also collected on users' demographic characteristics and use of the library. The results demonstrate that user satisfaction is potentially useful for evaluating the performance of specific services within a library. However, this measure should not be used to compare presumed levels of performance for libraries serving different communities. User satisfaction was found to be unrelated to the user's degree of library use. The authors conclude that given the complexity of human behavior, user satisfaction measures should be used with caution. (revised by A. Craig Hawbaker)

* Doelling, Donna L. 1993. Blueprint for performance assessment. *Medical Reference Services Quarterly* 12: 29–38.

> Doelling presents a clear, concise methodology for putting together a self-study plan for evaluating the effectiveness of library services. A "how to" outline is succinctly laid out, and each step in the outline is discussed, justified, and explained—down to establishing a time frame and mobilizing resources. Measurements of performance were established based on the well-defined mission statement of the university involved, the University of South Florida College of Medicine. A survey committee was formed, comprised of members of the Information Services Department. The survey was designed based on the committee's research on the subject. Adaptation of their findings to ensure the survey fit the goals and criteria of the study assured appropriate and usable results. A Likert-style rating scale was used. The survey return rate

was 79.5 percent, and Doelling explains how this high rate of return was achieved. A copy of the survey is included, as is a figure presenting survey response by user affiliation. All types of libraries considering performing an evaluation of services would benefit from the straightforward, intelligent, "how to" nature of this article. (annotated by Jeanette Moore Piquet)

Fairfax County Public Library. 1988. *Information services profile. Fairfax County Public Library.* Chicago: Public Library Association.

For six years in the mid-1980s, the Fairfax (Virginia) County Public Library (FCPL) system conducted an annual study to measure the extent and efficiency of the FCPL's information services. The methodology used was adapted from *Output Measures for Public Libraries* by Zweizig and Rodger. Data for fiscal year 1988 were gathered between October 5 and November 1, 1987, at all 23 branch libraries. All information requests received in person, by phone, and through the mail were counted. To obtain annual estimates, the researchers multiplied the number of information transactions during the survey period by 11.5 (rather than 12, to compensate for holidays and other closings). Of the estimated 1,943,000 information transactions handled during fiscal year 88, 42 percent were reference questions (ranging from 20 to 51 percent across the branches), and 58 percent were directional questions. All information transactions amounted to 2.76 per capita, including 1.17 reference requests per capita. The study also found that 15 percent of all reference questions were asked by children. Ninety percent of all reference questions were answered within one day. Although numerous quantified measures were taken to assess the extent of information services, only one data point (i.e., the reference fill rate) was used to measure the effectiveness of the information services. Appendix B contains the forms and procedures used to collect and tally the data. (revised by Tom Peters)

* Fink, Arlene, ed. 1995. *The survey kit.* 9 vols. Thousand Oaks, Calif.: Sage.

Vol. 1. *The survey handbook,* Arlene Fink. Vol. 2. *How to ask survey questions,* Arlene Fink. Vol. 3. *How to conduct self-administered and mail surveys,* Linda B. Bourque and Eve P. Fielder. Vol. 4. *How to conduct interviews by telephone and in person,* James H. Frey and Sabine Mertens Oishi. Vol. 5. *How to design surveys,* Arlene Fink.

Vol. 6. *How to sample in surveys,* Arlene Fink. Vol. 7. *How to measure survey reliability and validity,* Mark S. Litwin. Vol. 8. *How to analyze survey data,* Arlene Fink. Vol. 9. *How to report on surveys,* Arlene Fink.

> The titles in this nine-volume set can be consulted individually or read sequentially. They are arranged to approximate the steps taken in a survey project (e.g., the volume on designing the survey comes before the volume on analyzing the data). Taken together the survey kit provides a comprehensive, readable introduction to many of the issues faced by survey researchers. The editors employ a standard format throughout. Each volume in the kit includes a set of instructional objectives, sample surveys, exercises and answers, and annotated references. (annotated by Eric Novotny)

* Fink, Arlene, and Jacqueline Kosecoff. 1998. *How to conduct surveys: A step-by-step guide.* 2nd ed. Beverly Hills, Calif.: Sage.

> This brief book (103 pages) provides practical advice on designing, conducting, and interpreting surveys. General information about such major issues as question construction, sampling, ethics, and data analysis is provided. Given its brevity, the work necessarily covers many issues only briefly, and is most useful to beginning researchers looking for an easy-to-understand overview. One strength of this work is its design and layout: the authors make good use of charts, graphs, examples, and exercises to break up the text and illustrate key points. The second edition includes some discussion of interactive computer-assisted surveys, although the focus is more on using computers for data analysis than on how to conduct surveys electronically. (annotated by Eric Novotny)

Fisher, Kenneth, and Carlos Alexander. 1976. Survey of Olin Library users. In *User Surveys.* SPEC Kit 24. Washington, D.C.: Association of Research Libraries, Office of Management Studies.

> This study of when to distribute user surveys indicates that using exit surveys will lead to higher return rates. In a pilot test, Fisher and Alexander gave out fifty forms to library users as they entered the library, and fifty to those leaving the library. The entrance survey had a return rate of 52 percent, while the exit survey had a return rate of 80 percent. Using the latter method, the final study achieved a return rate of 97 percent. (revised by Tom Peters)

* Fowler, Floyd J., Jr. 1993. *Survey research methods.* 2nd ed. Applied Social Research Methods Series, vol. 1. Newbury Park, Calif.: Sage.

This second edition retains the overall goal of the first, to provide a summary of current knowledge on survey methods. It is not intended for statisticians or professional researchers. Basic information is provided on topics such as random sampling, question design, and methods of data collection. The newer edition includes more current references, a greater emphasis on machine-assisted surveys, and a chapter on the research and supervision of training interviewers. (annotated by Eric Novotny)

Giesbrecht, Walter. 1991. Staff resistance to library CD-ROM services. *CD-ROM Professional* 4: 34–38.

Giesbrecht summarizes and categorizes the responses of 25 respondents to a question posted about the reasons for resistance to CD-ROM services. The questions were posted to 1,400 to 1,500 potential respondents on PACS-L, an electronic discussion forum, and to members of the Canadian Library Association's CD-ROM interest group on Envoy 100, an electronic mail service in Canada. About sixty different reasons for resistance to technology are reduced to seven categories: psychological resistance, problems of multiple interfaces, increased costs, increased stress, time required to maintain CD-ROMs, hardware problems, and software issues. Giesbrecht argues that resistance to technology is an untapped source of information for library administrators and planners and points to the dangers of unanticipated and unplanned change. Resistance creates a healthy tension with progress that results in healthy growth. Most importantly, the author makes an excellent case for better planning, improved staff training, and a careful examination of what training needs library clientele may have, all well in the advance of the introduction of new technologies. Resistance to technological change is not irrational, but an opportunity to listen. Such resistance points to inadequacies in planning. (revised by Frank Elliott)

Gunning, Kathleen, and Kimberly Spyers-Duran. 1993. Evaluation of Reference Expert: An expert system of selecting reference sources. In *First preconference on research in reference effectiveness,* ed. Marjorie Murfin and Jo Bell Whitlatch. RASD Occasional Paper 16. Chicago: American Library Association, Reference and Adult Services Division.

The authors describe a survey questionnaire used to evaluate Reference Expert (RE), a database-selection expert system at the University of Houston Libraries. Questionnaires were placed in the reference area near networked CD-ROM and dedicated Reference Expert workstations. The survey asked for information such as respondents' familiarity with their current research topics, which affects their ability to use the tool effectively, as well as for their research habits before and after using the tool. The questionnaire confirmed the tool's ability to raise users' awareness of the range of information resources available to them, and results would be useful to the library in setting the appropriate balance of human and automated assistance. The survey content is somewhat dated, in that this iteration of RE navigates a pre-Web world of information. Modification of this questionnaire to test new electronic services would have to take this into account. Much current usability testing research stresses the need for "live" subjects; that favored method is not mentioned here but should not be ignored by developers. Because plans to enhance the RE interface are not tied to specific survey results, it is not always clear how the development team made decisions about necessary system enhancements. (revised by Jim Stemper)

Halperin, Michael, and Maureen Strazdon. 1980. Measuring students' preferences for reference services: A conjoint analysis. *Library Quarterly* 50: 208–224.

Reference services in a large university library are studied using a technique called conjoint analysis. Conjoint analysis is a method of measuring individual and group preferences to determine the relative importance of aspects of a particular service. In this study, students were asked to rank numerically twenty components of reference service. Students also supplied demographic data about themselves. The results indicated that accuracy and completeness of answers were most important to both graduate and undergraduate students. The length of the wait for service and the length of time to complete the service were ranked lowest. Differences among the various levels of service were not greatly significant. These data may be used in the development of user choice simulations to develop optimum service models. Conjoint analysis is a useful method by which to apply quantitative values to library services and to measure the benefit of such services to library patrons. (revised by Lorrie Knight)

* Harless, David W., and Frank R. Allen. (1999). Using the contingent valuation method to measure patron benefits of reference desk service in an academic library. *College & Research Libraries* 60: 56–69.

> The authors assert that an analysis of the benefits of reference services would serve better as an assessment method than an analysis of the costs. They also assert that only patrons are in a position to evaluate the worth of reference services in their own particular circumstances (e.g., opportunity cost of time, knowledge, other sources of assistance). The authors used a survey technique from the field of environmental economics known as the contingent valuation method to estimate the economic value that academic library patrons attach to reference desk service. Harless and Allen suggest that a comprehensive measure of the benefits patrons receive from a reference service program must include both use value (i.e., the usual concept of the benefit of a service) and option value (i.e., the benefit to potential users of knowing they have the option of using reference services). The authors contracted with Virginia Commonwealth University's Survey Research Lab to survey 382 students and full-time instructional faculty members at VCU—both users and non-users. Respondents were asked about various aspects of their willingness to pay for reference services. The data were gathered during the spring of 1997. Harless and Allen found that students and faculty members place a value on the current hours of reference desk service that exceeds actual cost estimates by a ratio of 3.5 to 1. (annotated by Tom Peters)

* Jardine, Carolyn W. 1995. Maybe the 55 percent rule doesn't tell the whole story: A user-satisfaction survey. *College & Research Libraries* 56: 477–485.

> Jardine discusses a user satisfaction survey conducted at the University Library of the University of Albany during the fall 1993 semester. Jardine found few studies of reference effectiveness focusing on the user as the primary source of data. This qualitative study is based on the premise that patrons will judge the reference service they receive not only by whether they get what they came in for, but also by the reference librarian's attitude, behavior, interest, and enthusiasm—key factors in patron satisfaction and willingness to return. The study included questions on behavioral characteristics of reference librarians, users' comfort with reference transactions, and whether patrons would return to the same librar-

ian. The design of the survey was based on forms developed by Murfin and Gugelchuk, Olson, and Durrance. Graduate students behind the reference desk handed out forms to voluntary patrons upon the completion of reference transactions. The one hundred completed surveys were distributed at different times of day and covered times when all reference librarians were working. Ninety-nine percent of respondents reported that they would return to the same reference librarian again. Patrons marked librarians highest on helpfulness and patience and lowest on self-confidence and enthusiasm. Jardine recommends that the library profession become more responsive to patrons' judgments of reference service because they are qualified to evaluate such performance. (annotated by Patricia L. Gregory and Razia Nanji)

King, Geraldine, and Suzanne H. Mahmoodi. 1991. Peer performance appraisal of reference librarians in a public library. In *Evaluation of public services and public service librarians*. Allerton Park Institute no. 32. Urbana-Champaign: University of Illinois, Graduate School of Library and Information Science.

> The authors describe an instrument designed to evaluate the performance of public reference librarians. The appraisal system, developed at the Ramsey County Public Library in Minnesota, includes a competency-based self-evaluation followed by a one-hour peer-group discussion. The reaction from staff has been mostly positive, and the system was still in use five years after it was introduced. The staff found it has improved both individual and group problem-solving and priority setting. The instrument could be adapted for use in academic libraries. The appendixes include the complete Self-Appraisal Form, as well as the Competency List, Factors Affecting Level of Performance (part of the self-evaluation), and Tips for Peer Evaluation Participants. (revised by Jim Stemper)

Lowenthal, Ralph A. 1990. Preliminary indications of the relationship between reference morale and performance. *RQ* 29: 380–393.

> Lowenthal conducted a study of 37 reference providers in seven public-service units in four Midwestern public libraries, each with less than 50,000 volumes. A questionnaire was designed that amalgamated a variety of recognized instruments for measuring morale, job satisfaction, and burnout. Although the sample size was not large, the findings suggest that the performance and success rates

of reference units, as measured by the Wisconsin-Ohio Reference Evaluation Program, are related to staff morale, feelings of emotional well-being, rapport with the head of reference, public relations, group cohesiveness, and the work environment. (revised by Tom Peters)

Murfin, Marjorie E., and Charles A. Bunge. 1988a. Paraprofessionals at the reference desk. *Journal of Academic Librarianship* 14: 10–14.

The authors used the Reference Transaction Assessment Instrument to evaluate the impact of paraprofessionals at the reference desk. One form was used for each reference transaction and consisted of 100 to 200 questions (dependent on participating libraries). The form had two parts—one for the staff member to complete and one for the user to complete. The study did not examine directional questions. There were 20 participating libraries and 1,607 transactions, of which 291 were categorized as paraprofessional-based, 1,240 as professional-based, and 76 as unidentified. The report looked at four response clusters: Question Answering Success, Quality and Amount of Assistance, Librarian-Patron Communication, and Other Factors. Based on their analysis of the data, Murfin and Bunge concluded that paraprofessionals were (1) more likely to give patrons a smaller amount of time per question, (2) less successful at directing patrons through a search, (3) less successful with underclass students, (4) less successful on complex questions, and (5) less aware of the patron's perceptions of success or of communication difficulties. Despite some methodological shortcomings, the article identifies key issues to be addressed in putting paraprofessionals at the reference desk. (revised by John Mess)

Murfin, Marjorie E., and Charles A. Bunge. 1988b. Responsible standards for reference service in Ohio public libraries. *Ohio Libraries* 1: 11–13.

This brief article reports on the Ohio Library Association's examination of public library reference standards that employ self-rating. A study utilizing the Reference Transaction Assessment Instrument showed little similarity between reference librarians' self-ratings when compared to success ratings reported by patrons. The authors conclude that self-rating is insufficient as a means of determining to what degree standards have been met. Three qualities of responsible standard-setting are recommended: obtaining and using normative data, selecting from a choice of objectives, and accounting for factors which may affect success of outcome. (revised by A. Craig Hawbaker)

Murfin, Marjorie, and Gary Gugelchuk. 1987. Development and testing of a Reference Transaction Assessment Instrument. *College & Research Libraries* 48: 314–338.

> The authors designed a reference assessment tool that articulated the outcome of reference activity in terms of patron reports of success. Fifteen academic libraries participated in the study, providing a set of 531 reference transactions with matching responses from both the patron and the reference provider. The patron questionnaire included fourteen questions that help to provide details of the reference interaction that may have an influence on patron satisfaction. The responses were analyzed in terms of thirty-five variables. The authors found that patron reports of success on factual questions did not differ significantly from results obtained via unobtrusive observation. The Reference Transaction Assessment Instrument has been widely used in academic and public libraries ranging in size from 33,000 volumes to over 4 million volumes. It has proven to be a reliable and valid instrument for measuring the accuracy of reference services. (revised by Tom Peters and Eric Novotny)

* Murfin, Marjorie, and Lubomyr R. Wynar. 1977. *Reference service: An annotated bibliographic guide*. Littleton, Colo.: Libraries Unlimited.

> These publications provide easy and convenient access to early studies using surveys for reference assessment. The 1977 edition of this bibliography covers literature from 1876 to 1975. The 1984 supplement covers publications from 1976 to 1982. Together the two bibliographies provide the most comprehensive overview of works related to reference assessment up to 1982. The supplement alone contains 1,668 annotated citations divided into 14 chapters. The bibliography includes books, articles, dissertations, conference proceedings, and other formats. Only English-language citations are included. (annotated by Eric Novotny)

Nitecki, Danuta. 1993. User criteria for evaluating the effectiveness of the online catalog. In *First preconference on research in reference effectiveness*, ed. Marjorie Murfin and Jo Bell Whitlatch. RASD Occasional Paper 16. Chicago: American Library Association, Reference and Adult Services Division.

Nitecki's study had two goals: to better understand the method of naturalistic inquiry (a type of qualitative assessment), and to investigate the feasibility of this approach as a means of soliciting user criteria of quality library services. Only one library attribute—the online catalog—was studied. Nitecki argues that because criteria for evaluating the effectiveness of a library service are constructs residing in the minds of library users, and are not grounded in a single transcendent reality, naturalistic inquiry is an appropriate assessment technique. Naturalistic inquiry assumes that truth changes and is context-based. Nitecki studied a group of 24 in-library online catalog users (both novice and experienced users) at the University of Maryland at College Park. After completing an online catalog search session, users were approached and asked to be interviewed. The ten- to twenty-minute interviews were audiotaped, and written field notes were taken. Data were collected between November 16 and December 9, 1991. The effectiveness factors included ease of use, search strategy, selection information, location information, and the content scope of the online catalog. Ease of use and location information were ranked most important most often. One of the strengths of this method is the integration of the interviewer's expertise into the data-gathering process as a means to probe more deeply into the participants' environment. (revised by Tom Peters)

* Oppermann, Martin. 1995. E-mail surveys: Potentials and pitfalls. *Marketing Research* 7 (3): 28–33.

Oppermann reports on the results of an e-mail survey distributed to members of the Association of American Geographers. Randomly selected members received the survey either via e-mail or regular mail. Based on the responses, the authors conclude that the main advantage of e-mail surveys is the rapid response rate. Over 20 percent of those contacted responded within two days. Disadvantages such as incorrect e-mail addresses and problems with older e-mail programs are discussed. (annotated by Eric Novotny)

* Parker, June D. 1996. Evaluating documents reference service and the implications for improvement. *Journal of Government Information* 23: 49–70.

A study of reference service at the government documents desk at East Carolina University is outlined. The author discusses using the Wisconsin-Ohio Reference Evaluation Program (WOREP) to evaluate the effectiveness of the documents staff in answering questions. Parker provides data from prior studies on use and users of government information, background on WOREP, and information about the library and its particular population. Results from the WOREP study were high for this library, and may suggest that having a separate documents desk produces a much higher success rate with documents-related questions, but the very small sample size suggests further study might be warranted. (annotated by Paula Contreras)

* Parten, Mildred. 1950. *Surveys, polls, and samples: Practical procedures*. New York: Harper.

This work must now be used with some caution, since research practices have changed over the years, but it remains one of the standards in the field. In one large volume (624 pages) all of the major topics related to survey research are clearly discussed. The emphasis is on the practical rather than the theoretical. Professional readings are not ignored, but they are supplemented by real-world advice from the author based on her experiences as a researcher. This work will be of particular interest to those with a historical bent. In addition to providing a contemporary account of research methods of the 1950s, there is a lengthy overview of the history of surveys in the United States. (annotated by Eric Novotny)

* Robinson, David, and Val Reed. 1998. *The A-Z of social research jargon*. Aldershot, Eng.: Ashgate.

This book is written to aid the complete novice researcher. Although aimed at a health sciences audience, its basic approach makes it suitable for all fields. A brief "everyday" definition is provided for each term, followed by a more detailed explanation of the term's use in research practice. (annotated by Eric Novotny)

* Roselle, Ann, and Steven Neufeld. 1998. The utility of electronic mail follow-ups for library research. *Library and Information Science Research* 20: 153–161.

The authors conducted a research project to compare the use of e-mail and paper-based mail as follow-ups to a paper-based mailed questionnaire. The researchers chose to use e-mail, not as a method for distributing the original survey, but as a communication method during the follow-up mailing stage. In May 1997 a survey was mailed to a national random sample of 224 academic librarians assigned to work with federal government depository collections. The survey was designed to elicit answers about how Internet-related technologies affected the respondents' relationships with fellow workers. Identical wording was used for both the postcard and e-mail follow-up messages, and the researchers tried to make the messages arrive at the two groups of subjects on the same day. The overall response rate was 83 percent. The authors found that, as a follow-up method, e-mail was as effective as postal mail, in terms of both the speed and size of the survey response. They concluded that, as a communication medium, e-mail can be used effectively during the data collection process, especially for survey research projects. When the speed and cost efficiencies of e-mail are factored in, the use of e-mail for library research and assessment becomes more attractive. (annotated by Tom Peters and Paula Contreras)

* Schaefer, David R., and Don A. Dillman. 1998. Development of a standard e-mail methodology. *Public Opinion Quarterly* 62: 378–397+.

The authors conducted a controlled experiment to judge the effects of different delivery modes on survey response rates. Their results indicate that using a mixed mode, whereby respondents who are inaccessible via e-mail receive the survey in print, can increase response rates. Those responding electronically did so more rapidly, and more completely. The use of prenotices, or electronic cover letters, to request participation was generally found to increase response rate over those who were not given advance notice of the survey being sent. (annotated by Eric Novotny)

* Schuldt, Barbara, and Jeffrey Totten. 1994. Electronic mail vs. mail survey response rates. *Marketing Research* 6: 36–39.

The authors compare the response rates from electronic mail surveys with those of mail questionnaires distributed to management information systems (MIS) and marketing faculty at U.S. colleges and universities. The response rate for electronic mail was found to be low. Those who chose to respond to the e-mail survey were found to have a greater interest in technology than the average respondent. The authors nevertheless conclude that further study of electronic mail surveying is warranted, given the medium's potential. (annotated by Eric Novotny)

Strong, Gary E. 1980. Evaluating the reference product. *RQ* 19: 367–372.

Strong attempts to define and evaluate the reference product. In early 1978, the Policy Research Group of the Consortium for Public Library Innovation undertook a pilot project to measure and evaluate adult reference services at the Washington State Library. Users were queried and classified based on the primary purpose of their visit to the library: job-related purposes, educational or learning purposes, and leisure or personal purposes. Data were collected by questionnaire. Strong notes that a good evaluation program should recognize that library staff, patrons, and management should have the opportunity to review and apply this assessment information in differing ways. A "user ticket" was used to collect basic demographic and intentional information from all users entering the library on the day of the study. The Statistical Package for the Social Sciences (SPSS) software was used to manipulate the data and generate reports. The findings indicate that 40 percent of library users requested assistance from staff members, 71 percent of these found what they sought, and 81 percent were satisfied with the services they received. Data were also gathered via "patterns of information request" forms completed by the library staff. Each reference staff member was also interviewed by Strong to learn the attitudes and opinions of reference providers about the quality of the reference service provided. (revised by Tom Peters)

* Suskie, Linda. 1992. *Questionnaire survey research: What works.* 2nd ed. Tallahassee, Fla.: American Association for Institutional Research.

This book provides a basic introduction to survey research intended for novice researchers. One of its strengths is that it is written in a very informative, easy-to-understand style, making it an excellent source to consult if this is your first research project. The emphasis is on practical advice for those who are not professional surveyors. While not written for libraries or librarians, the material presented is adaptable to almost any setting. A question-and-answer format is utilized, making it possible to quickly zero in on sections that address specific research questions. The author walks the reader through all stages of the research process, beginning with planning the survey and ending with reporting the results. Appendixes provide sample time lines, cover letters and surveys, and suggestions for locating additional information. (annotated by Eric Novotny)

* Tse, Alan C. B. 1998. Comparing the response rate, response speed, and response quality of two methods of sending out questionnaires: e-mail versus mail. *Journal of the Marketing Research Society* 40: 353–361.

> Tse presents the results of a survey conducted using names selected from the telephone directory of The Chinese University of Hong Kong. The author found substantial differences between the surveys distributed via e-mail and regular mail. The response time for mail surveys was nearly six days longer on average. However, response rates for the paper survey were much higher than for the e-mail surveys, 52 percent to 7 percent. Response quality was found to be equivalent for both survey methods. The article includes a literature review of recent studies on e-mail surveys. (annotated by Eric Novotny)

Van House, Nancy A., and Thomas Childers. 1993. *The public library effectiveness study: The complete report.* Chicago: American Library Association.

> The goal of this nationwide study was to define the effectiveness of public libraries as social institutions. Van House and Childers developed a list of 61 indicators of public library effectiveness, then surveyed seven key internal and external constituencies (i.e., library service staff, library managers, trustees, library users, the members of library friends' groups, local officials, and community leaders) about the usefulness of the indicators. A regionalized sampling from mid-sized public libraries was taken, and all libraries serving populations of at least one million were automatically included. Data were collected via mailed questionnaires. Three separate survey instruments posed the questions, which fell into four categories: (1) preference for (or usefulness of) indicators, (2) performance of the library in question on those indicators, (3) the roles or domains of the library, and (4) selected demographics of the library. Respondents to the survey rated all 61 indicators of effectiveness on a 5-point Likert scale. Several of the effectiveness indicators are related to the assessment of reference services, such as the percentage of reference questions answered, the helpfulness, courteousness, and concern of the staff, speed of

service, the quality of the staff (in terms of education and talent), service to special groups, and staff morale. The return rate was 90 percent, and over 2,400 responses were received. Library managers and service staff ranked the reference role as the most important of eight basic roles for public libraries. (revised by Tom Peters)

* Wallace, Linda K. 1994. Customer feedback: How to get it. *College & Research Libraries News* 55: 64–65.

Wallace provides an overview of the American Library Association-designed Customer Satisfaction Survey, a tool intended for use by all types of libraries. Her article includes brief tips on administering a customer service survey. (annotated by Eric Novotny)

Weech, Terry L., and Herbert Goldhor. 1984. Reference clientele and the reference transaction in five Illinois public libraries. *Library and Information Science Research* 6: 21–42.

Patrons from five public libraries in Illinois were surveyed to learn how they perceived a recent reference transaction. The data were collected from library staff and 125 reference clients. The reference staff completed a brief form describing the question, and the volunteer patron participants received a questionnaire afterward in the mail. Patrons were queried about their background, the origin of their question, their satisfaction with the answer, and how and if they used the information. This study yielded a number of results, including noncorrelation between the origin of the question and satisfaction with the outcome, a gender difference in the origin of questions, and a high customer-satisfaction rate. (revised by Laura Dale Bischof)

* Weible, Rick, and John Wallace. 1998. Cyber research: The impact of the Internet on data collection. *Marketing Research* 10 (3): 19–24+.

This article compares four methods of data collection: mail, fax, e-mail, and Web form. Based on the results of a survey conducted in each medium, the authors conclude that the new methods (fax, e-mail, and Web form) are significantly faster than paper forms, and can be conducted at a cheaper cost. Mail forms, while slower and more expensive, did achieve much higher response rates. The authors argue that this advantage is outweighed by the ease of increasing the sample size for electronic surveys. Those desiring more responses can easily send out many more surveys in e-mail than they could reasonably do with a paper survey. (annotated by Eric Novotny)

Westbrook, Lynn. 1984. Catalog failure and reference service. *RQ* 24: 82–90.

Westbrook attempts to specify and explore the relationship between users of the library catalog and their use of reference services, including what prevents card catalog users from approaching reference staff. Over a nine-week period a questionnaire was designed, refined, and eventually tested in two different formats. Data were collected at the Regenstein Library at the University of Chicago over a period of eighteen hours spread over six days. A twenty-question, Likert-type questionnaire was randomly distributed to 1,086 people at the entrance to the library, and 663 questionnaires were returned to a box positioned near the distribution point. Barriers to the use of reference service were divided into attitudinal problems (willingness to assist, helpfulness or competence, busyness, awkwardness in approaching, and rudeness) and informational problems (awareness of common reference tools, catalog scope, and knowledge of reference services). Westbrook found that a small but meaningful proportion of patrons are not finding what they are looking for in the catalog, and that academic level does strongly affect their success rate. The barriers to utilization of reference services by catalog users were not primarily attitudinal, but rather based on a lack of accurate information concerning the location, function, and identification of reference librarians. Reference librarians at the desk need to appear less involved with other work and more available to patrons. (revised by Tom Peters)

Whitlatch, Jo Bell. 1990a. Reference service effectiveness. *RQ* 30: 205–220.

An exploratory study of reference success was conducted in five northern California libraries. Sixty-two librarians participated by asking every fifth reference patron to complete a questionnaire. Librarians also completed questionnaires about the same reference questions. Data were collected for variables such as the patron's perception of success or failure in locating needed information, and the librarian's job satisfaction, time constraints, and opportunities for feedback from the patron. Results showed that the most important factors related to reference success were feedback (librarians asking patrons if they found the information they needed), service orientation of the librarian, and task-related knowledge of the librarian. Whitlatch concluded that it is important to study reference encounters from both the librarian's and the patron's perspective. (revised by Susan Clark)

Whitlatch, Jo Bell. 1990b. *The role of the academic reference librarian.* New York: Greenwood.

Whitlatch examines key factors related to successful reference practices in academic libraries. Data were collected from 257 reference encounters involving 62 reference librarians at five academic libraries. Both librarians and patrons completed a questionnaire. User and librarian feedback, the interpersonal skills of the librarian, and the librarian's task-related knowledge were found to be the most significant variables affecting service outcomes. (revised by Eric Novotny)

Willett, Holly G. 1992. Designing an evaluation instrument: The Environment Rating Scale "in process." *Journal of Youth Services in Libraries* 5: 165–173.

Willett describes the development of an assessment instrument called the "Environment Rating Scale for Public Library Children's Services" (E-Scale). The E-Scale assumes that the goal of children's services is to enhance child development, and that having an environment that supports children will enable public libraries to achieve their desired impact. The design goal was to develop an instrument that children's librarians could use to evaluate their own services, and that researchers, planners, architects, and consultants could use to evaluate children's library services on a regional or national basis. A public library's "environment" includes the physical facilities, staff behavior and attitudes, collections, policies, and procedures. Willett submitted the first version of the instrument to a panel of eleven children's services experts to test for validity, defined here as confirmation that the desired qualities are being measured, and that what is being measured is appropriate and important to the mission of the library. A seven-point Likert-type scale was used for the forty-four items on the first draft. The first draft was field-tested in nine public libraries in Wisconsin and California. The second draft contained over twice as many items, and three separate scales were devised: an early childhood scale, a middle childhood scale, and a small libraries scale, which selectively combined items from the two other scales in order to be more useful to libraries with three or fewer staff members. The scales were again field-tested, and third drafts were formulated. (revised by Tom Peters)

* Young, Michael. 1992. *Dictionary of polling: The language of contemporary opinion research*. New York: Greenwood.

>Young defines the most important terms in public opinion research. Brief, readable definitions are provided for approximately four hundred terms. Each entry includes cross-references and citations to works containing more information. The emphasis is on commonly used terms readers are likely to encounter frequently. Specialized and highly technical terms are excluded. Each entry includes citations to the literature. (annotated by Eric Novotny)

See also the annotations in the following sections of part IV:

Chapter 1—Quality of Reference Service Products: Van House et al. (1987), Van House, Weil, and McClure (1990);

Chapter 2: Zweizig et al. (1996);

Chapter 3: Baker and Lancaster (1991), Busha and Harter (1980), Evaluation of Reference and Adult Services Committee (1995), White and Abels (1995);

Chapter 5: Alafiatoayo, Yip, and Blunden-Ellis (1996).

CHAPTER 5
OBSERVATION

* Alafiatoayo, Benjamin O., Yau J. Yip, and John C. P. Blunden-Ellis. 1996. Reference transaction and the nature of the process for general reference assistance. *Library and Information Science Research* 18: 357–384.

>The authors studied the general reference process and the role of reference librarians in academic libraries in the United Kingdom. Methods included sending questionnaires to reference librarians in twenty-two academic libraries, using unobtrusive observation of reference transactions in two university libraries, and conducting pretests to determine a structured observation schedule. Observation spanned four weeks at the busiest periods of the day and resulted in a ranking of key reference activities. This type of study could be conducted in public libraries as well as academic ones. The authors conclude that observations and surveys revealed that the task deemed most important for reference librarians is the "identi-

fication and selection of sources that could answer users' queries and solve their informational problems." This process of choosing appropriate sources represents the professional expertise of the reference librarian and is defined as a "select strategy." The authors recommend including the select strategy in any future model of the reference process, and they intend to pursue this emphasis in the next stage of their research. (annotated by Patricia L. Gregory)

Arrigona, Daniel, and Eleanor Mathews. 1988. A use study of an academic library reference collection. *RQ* 28: 71–81.

Arrigona and Mathews studied the use of the reference collection at the Iowa State University library. Data were collected during four weeks of the 1986 spring semester. They analyzed the materials used both by librarians responding to reference requests and by users seeking information on their own. Tally sheets were used to record librarian use of the reference collection, and the table-count method was used as an indirect indication of patron use of the collection. The authors hypothesized that librarians and patrons use the reference collection differently, and that use varies across Library of Congress subject classifications and material types. The research revealed that the L (education) classification range had the highest use index (i.e., the number of uses divided by the number of volumes), followed by the A range and telephone directories. The findings indicated that not only do unassisted users consult different classification areas than do librarians seeking information, but that library users in the fields of science and technology find their own reference materials without a librarian's assistance. They note that few reference assessment projects have focused on the resources and materials involved in providing reference service. As a statistical foundation, a reference collection-use study could be used to manage reference collections, formulate departmental budgets, and plan user services. (revised by Tom Peters)

Childers, Thomas. 1980. The test of reference. *Library Journal* 105: 924–928.

Childers summarizes the results of unobtrusive testing at fifty-seven libraries on Long Island, New York. The same set of twenty questions was asked at each library at different times over a period of six months. The questions were of four types: (1) basic facts, (2) bibliographic information, (3) local social services or government inquiries, and (4) "escalators," questions to test negotiation skills. The results indicated that when an answer was given, only 47 percent were correct. Only 20 percent of the librarians fully negotiated the question. About one-third of nonanswered questions were directed to an external agency where the answer was found. No library scored perfectly, and every library had some success. Reference collection size and staffing did not affect performance. Childers suggests that the results reflect many local factors. To improve performance, library managers should define their library's service orientation, set performance measures and standards, formalize policies for handling inquiries, and establish the level of service the user may expect. (revised by John Mess)

* Czopek, Vanessa. 1998. Using mystery shoppers to evaluate customer service in the public library. *Public Libraries* 37: 370–375.

Czopek describes how the Stanislaus County (California) Free Library used "mystery shoppers" as a method of unobtrusive observation to establish benchmarks for customer service in the main library and the twelve branches. The annual strategic plans of all Stanislaus County departments, including those of the County Library, are related to the county goals of excellent customer service. The county adopted the Malcolm Baldridge Award criteria to help county departments assess how well customer service goals were being met. The large downtown Stanislaus County Library in Modesto participated in the Modesto Chamber of Commerce program to have mystery shoppers rate the library service. Information gleaned from the mystery shoppers was useful when assessing customer service trends, staff service attitudes, and the effectiveness of staff training programs. The results were shared with the entire library staff, and a business consultant was brought in to conduct a series of customer service workshops for the staff. Five alliterative terms that define good customer service are "prompt, perceptive, personal, prepared, and positive." After the original mystery shop at the downtown library in 1996, a better assessment tool that was specific to the library setting was developed and administered through mystery shopping at the twelve branch libraries. For the branch libraries, each mystery shopper received a separate reference question to ask at each site visited. The article includes the Modesto Chamber of Commerce Service Evaluation, Branch Library Mystery Shopper Questionnaire, and Stanislaus County Free Library Customer Service Standards. (annotated by Tom Peters and Jeanette Moore Piquet)

ANNOTATED BIBLIOGRAPHY

* Dewdney, Patricia, and Catherine Sheldrick Ross. 1994. Flying a light aircraft: Reference service evaluation from a user's viewpoint. *RQ* 34: 217–230.

> This unobtrusive study followed the pursuits of 77 graduate library school students who visited an academic or public library of their choice in order to ask a reference question that personally mattered to them. Each user completed a written account of the reference encounter and outcome, including willingness to return to that same librarian on another occasion with a different question. The results, which were tabulated and analyzed using the Statistical Package for the Social Sciences (SPSS) software, showed contrasting differences in users' accounts of the "most helpful" and "least helpful" reference service. The four reference behaviors that most affected users' perception of service were the anonymity or identification of a professional reference librarian; the lack of a reference interview; unmonitored referrals; and the lack of follow-up questions. Remedies for these problems are suggested. As in Durrance's 1989 article, only about 60 percent of the users expressed a willingness to return to the same librarian again for a different question. No significant differences were found between academic and public libraries. (annotated by A. Craig Hawbaker)

Durrance, Joan C. 1989. Reference success: Does the 55 percent rule tell the whole story? *Library Journal* 114: 31–36.

> This study used an unobtrusive methodology to test the impact of the reference environment on the willingness of patrons to ask follow-up questions of the same staff member. This is in contrast to studies that use accuracy as the main determinant of reference service success. Library school students observed 266 reference interviews in public, academic, and special libraries in several states. The participants approached reference staff and posed questions significant to their own lives. The library school students recorded their questions and collected data about the staff member's activities at the desk before their interview and the staff member's interpersonal skills. The student participants were also asked to guess whether they were served by a librarian, assistant, or student. Sixty-three percent of the students were willing to return to the same staff member with a follow-up question. Factors affecting their decision were the activity and body language of the staff member upon approach, name identification, and interpersonal signals such as friendliness and interest. (revised by Laura Dale Bischof)

* Durrance, Joan. 1995. Factors that influence reference success: What makes questioners willing to return? *Reference Librarian,* nos. 49/50: 243–265.

> Rather than focusing on the accuracy of question answering, as most reference assessment studies since 1970 have done, Durrance points out the benefits of utilizing other measures. Her "Willingness to Return Study" is an obtrusive measure of reference success used since 1986 in over twelve hundred interviews in public and academic libraries. It is designed to determine if the person who asks the question would return to the same librarian with another question at a later time. The user's willingness to return may be influenced by the librarian's (1) activity and posture when approached, (2) anonymity, (3) first words or opening statement, (4) question negotiation and interview skills, (5) interpersonal skills, (6) ability to determine need, (7) length of interaction, (8) follow-up, and (9) form of closure. Factors associated with the most successful reference transactions (users said they would return over 80 percent of the time) include the use of open questions, determining the need behind a question, good listening skills, and appearing interested in the question. Each area examined here is ripe for further study and assessment in both public and academic libraries. Short case studies and statistical results are included. (annotated by A. Craig Hawbaker)

* Elzy, Cheryl Asper, et al. 1991. Evaluating reference service in a large academic library. *College & Research Libraries* 52: 454–465.

> Several researchers at Milner Library at Illinois State University conducted an unobtrusive study in the spring of 1989 that measured the ability of professional librarians to deal with factual reference questions. The main objectives of the study were to ascertain the quality of reference service by estimating the probability of a patron receiving an accurate answer to factual questions; to identify potential problem areas of service; to identify conditions under which librarians perform well; and to identify ways to improve reference service. The study was designed to evaluate library faculty members on attitudinal characteristics and on whether or not they were able to provide complete and correct answers to reference queries. Students were recruited as proxies to pose questions to nineteen reference librarians in five departments. A total of 190 test questions were devised, which could be answered by the collection. Each proxy was given an evaluation form to record the test ques-

tion and the answer given by the librarian, as well as a space for re-cording observations about each librarian's attitude and demeanor. The proxies also were encouraged to provide general comments. A scoring procedure was devised for various levels of "correctness" of answers and behavior of librarians, taking into account other variables such as time of day. The survey revealed that accuracy was only slightly associated with attitudinal scores (i.e., answering a question correctly did not necessarily correlate with how the sub-jects perceived they were treated). (annotated by Razia Nanji)

Gers, Ralph, and Lillie J. Seward. 1985. Improving reference performance: Results of a statewide study. *Library Journal* 110: 32–35.

> Gers and Seward summarize the findings of a statewide study of reference service conducted by the Public Library Branch of the Division of Library Development Services, Maryland State Depart-ment of Education. Using unobtrusive testing, they asked a set of forty questions at sixty library units. The questions were of two types: direct (specific answer) and negotiated (the actual need must be identified). The responses were classed into ten degrees of cor-rectness. Other variables, such as collection size, reference staff-ing, degree of privacy, and respondent's behaviors were also recorded. The statistical analysis showed that librarian behaviors most significantly determine the correctness of the response. Over-all a user is likely to receive a correct answer to a moderately diffi-cult question only 55 percent of the time. Specific behaviors, however, raised this probability significantly. The study identified six steps to improve performance: (1) elicit the specific question, (2) determine the intent in the user's question, (3) show attention and concern for the user and the question (comfortable in the ref-erence process), (4) check to see if the user's question has been answered, (5) cite the source or point out the answer when re-sponding to user, and (6) become familiar with basic information sources. (revised by John Mess)

Halldorsson, Egill A., and Marjorie E. Murfin. 1977. The performance of professionals and non-professionals in the reference interview. *College & Research Libraries* 38: 385–395.

> An unobtrusive study was undertaken at two medium-sized Mid-western university libraries. The study examined the relative suc-cess of professional and nonprofessional reference staff in probing

beyond indirect questions and detecting and correcting faulty information in reference questions. One library's reference service was staffed entirely by professional librarians, while the other library had an information center staffed by nonprofessionals with access to subject specialists. Twenty-five different reference interviews were conducted by seven investigators in each of the two libraries. The questions used in the interviews were drawn from Murfin's reference experience. The results indicated that professional librarians did much better than nonprofessionals both in probing behind indirect questions involving broad subjects (91 versus 73 percent) and in indirect questions involving the wrong type of source mentioned (90 versus 50 percent). Librarians were also more effective in correcting faulty information in questions involving a misspelling (75 versus 25 percent) and in correcting generally faulty information used as part of a question (38 versus 16 percent). Lack of orientation, less personal subject knowledge, and less knowledge of reference sources appeared to be the primary reasons why nonprofessionals performed poorly. Professional failure was more often due to reluctance to undertake difficult interviews and to lack of time to conduct either a proper interview or to carefully examine reference sources. (revised by Frank Elliott)

Harris, Roma M., and B. Gillian Michell. 1986. The social context of reference work: Assessing the effects of gender and communication skill on observers' judgments of competence. *Library and Information Science Research* 8: 85–101.

Harris and Michell focused on the social aspects of reference interactions; i.e., how conceptions of gender, physical appearance, and communication skills affect the interaction. Previous studies had made suggestions for improving interpersonal skills, but few yielded empirical data. More than 300 adult public library patrons participated in the study; each participant viewed one videotaped in-depth reference interview. After viewing the videotapes, the observers rated the librarian's behavior on a 24-item scale and completed a test of sex-role identity. Librarians who displayed non-verbal warmth, such as smiling, were viewed as the most competent and professional. Participants responded most positively to librarians who walked patrons through the research process when those patrons were not the same gender as the participants. Thus it appears that gender plays a role in how patrons view the reference interaction. (revised by Laura Dale Bischof)

Havener, W. Michael. 1990. Answering ready reference questions: Print versus online. *Online* 14: 22–28.

> In a controlled experiment, Havener compared the success of librarians responding to a set of questions using exclusively print or online sources. Twelve questions, half of which were conceptual and half factual, were devised and presented to sixty-eight librarians. Half of the librarians used online search services to respond. The other half of them used print sources. For conceptual questions, online sources proved to be faster and the resulting citations more relevant. For factual questions, print sources proved to be faster. There was no significant difference in the accuracy rate for print versus online for the factual questions. The results of this study suggest that the selection of the best resource format could lead to significant time savings for reference librarians. Patrons will also benefit from the librarian's selection of the most efficient and accurate resource. (revised by Lorrie Knight)

Havener, W. Michael. 1993. Print, online, or ondisc: The influence of format on the outcome of searches by graduate students. In *First preconference on research in reference effectiveness,* ed. Marjorie Murfin and Jo Bell Whitlatch. RASD Occasional Paper 16. Chicago: American Library Association, Reference and Adult Services Division.

> Havener compared the efficiency (time required to complete a transaction), success (recall, precision, and satisfaction), and effectiveness (number of relevant citations per minute) of print versus CD-ROM and online versions of *Psychological Abstracts and Sociological Abstracts*. The study was conducted in 1992 with forty-one graduate students in two graduate library and information-studies classes. The study was designed so that each student searched the same eighteen questions. The question order and type of search system used (print, CD-ROM, and online) were randomized. The results of the study were analyzed using an analysis of variance in which the search system used and type of question (conceptual versus factual) served as the categorical independent variables and efficiency, success, and effectiveness served as the dependent variables. Overall, the study showed that there were few interaction effects between search mode and type of question. The effects were main effects as opposed to interactions. Major findings were that for conceptual searches, both online and CD-ROM outperformed print in every way except for precision. For factual questions, the study showed that for author searches, the three search systems were roughly

equivalent. For title searches, print was the least desirable of the search systems. (revised by Frank Elliott)

Haynes, R. Brian, K. Ann McKibbon, Cynthia J. Walker, Nancy Ryan, Dorothy Fitzgerald, and Michael F. Ramsden. 1990. Online access to MEDLINE in clinical settings: A study of use and usefulness. *Annals of Internal Medicine* 112: 78–84.

> Self-service access to MEDLINE using GRATEFUL MED software was made available to physicians, trainees, and attending staff in a clinical setting at a university medical center. The 158 participants were offered a two-hour introduction and two hours of free search time. For each search conducted, a computer program recorded the user's identification and the search question. Search transactions were recorded automatically. These data, in conjunction with follow-up interviews and comparisons of the same search question executed by more expert searchers, allowed researchers to assess the frequency, patterns, purposes, and success of use. Eighty-one percent of participants performed searches at a mean rate of 2.7 searches per month. Compared to expert searchers, participants retrieved 55 percent as many relevant articles. However, clinicians with more searching experience performed as well as librarians. The authors conclude that end-user MEDLINE searching in clinical settings is feasible. However, inexperienced searchers search inefficiently and miss many relevant citations. Further studies are needed to assess the impact of searching on physician performance and patient care. (revised by A. Craig Hawbaker)

* Head, Michael C., and Rita Marcella. 1993. A testing question: The quality of reference services in Scottish public libraries. *Library Review* 42 (6): 7–13.

> Head and Marcella wanted to discover in more detail the elements within the reference process that were failing. They undertook an unobtrusive study of reference service in fifteen Scottish libraries. The study was designed so that the results could be compared with earlier research by D. House (1974, *Library Association Record* 76: 222–223) and P. Lea and L. Jackson (1988, *Library Association Record* 90: 582, 585). The sole question asked for biographical information about a public figure recently in the news, who already had written an autobiography. They found that central reference libraries in major cities did not respond well as a group to the question. In only one instance was something like a reference inter-

view conducted. The reference providers often concentrated on a specific category of material, such as journal articles or reference works. On only three occasions (out of fifteen) was any attempt made to evaluate the results of the search or to check whether the results satisfied the information need. Head and Marcella concluded that most reference librarians do not lack communication and interpersonal skills. Rather, most of the reference providers failed to exhibit a sense that the users themselves had anything to contribute to the reference process. (annotated by Tom Peters)

Hernon, Peter, and Charles R. McClure. 1986a. The quality of academic and public library reference service provided for NTIS products and services: Unobtrusive test results. *Government Information Quarterly* 3: 117–132.

Unobtrusive testing was used to collect data about reference accuracy in twelve government depository libraries. The focus of the questions concerned National Technical Information Service (NTIS) products and services. The objectives of the study were to determine the accuracy of answers to factual and bibliographic questions, to identify the factors that contributed to accuracy, and to compare the results by library type. The authors' hypotheses were that librarians associate government publications with the Government Printing Office and not the NTIS, that librarians infrequently use referral as a response strategy, and that reference success does not vary by type of library. Library students serving as proxies posed a series of carefully selected and pretested questions. Results indicated that the accuracy rate was less than 50 percent and was higher in academic libraries. Overall, unfamiliarity with the NTIS was the predominant factor in the failure to answer questions correctly. Referral, in particular to the NTIS itself, would have improved the accuracy rate, but was rarely done. The results suggest that reference personnel in depository libraries need more training in the role of the NTIS as a government publisher and in the use of indexing materials. Library staff should also be encouraged to make effective use of referrals when answering patrons' questions. (revised by Lorrie Knight)

Hernon, Peter, and Charles R. McClure. 1986b. Unobtrusive testing: The 55 percent rule. *Library Journal* 111: 37–41.

The authors report the methodology and results of extending unobtrusive reference testing to government documents reference. The sample included 26 libraries, 13 academic and 13 public, 10 from the West, 8 from the South, and 8 from the Midwest. The study compares reference accuracy findings for academic and public libraries, reference departments and government documents departments, and libraries by region. Fifteen questions were administered at each library in-person by proxies for a total of 390 questions asked during the period from March through June 1985. Participants in the study answered 61.8 percent of the questions correctly. From August to December 1985, the test was readministered at six of the original libraries with almost identical results. There were no statistically significant differences between the correct fill rate and either the type of library or the geographic region. Government documents departments answered 64.6 percent of the questions correctly, compared to 59.1 percent at general reference departments—a significant difference. Other noteworthy results include the short duration of most interactions (81.5 percent lasted five minutes or less), lack of referral to other sources, and lack of staff understanding of where library collections are listed. The authors argue for incorporating more formal methods of evaluation in library reference services to improve the quality of reference services. (revised by Frank Elliott)

Hernon, Peter, and Charles R. McClure. 1987. Quality of data issues in unobtrusive testing of library reference service: Recommendations and strategies. *Library and Information Science Research* 9: 77–93.

The authors explain the importance of three key links that are essential for the successful completion of unobtrusive testing of reference accuracy: reliability (stability and consistency of measurement), validity (both internal and external), and utility (application, impact, and usefulness of findings). In addition, any information collected must also have value, which means both sufficiency (is the measure an adequate reflection of what is being measured?) and practicality (is the information accessible and timely?). They argue for collecting information that is useful for library decision-making, planning, and evaluation. A table is included, where these key links and value are listed in one column, followed by possible actions to improve them in the next column. Links in the research chain need to be firmly secured so that the research is useful and hard to doubt in the decision-making context. The authors make a convincing case that the library profession must address the issue of assessing quality for a broad range of services offered by libraries.

Unobtrusive testing is viewed as a technique that can be applied to a much broader range of library services beyond reference. High-quality information services and effective interventions to improve services should be possible if a commitment is made to regular assessment. Ongoing evaluation is seen as an essential role of library management. (revised by Frank Elliott)

Hunter, Rhonda. 1991. Successes and failures of patrons searching the online catalog at a large academic library: A transaction log analysis. *RQ* 30: 395–402.

Hunter studied the Bibliographic Information System (BIS) online catalog at North Carolina State University at Raleigh. The project focused on failure rates, usage patterns, and causes of problems. The transaction logs included the terminal used, the date and time of the transaction, the type of search, and the search string, but not the number of hits retrieved, nor the type of screen displayed in response to the search. A total of 4,108 transactions generated at 15 of the 28 terminals in the library were captured between October 22 and 28, 1989. Multiple, identical, sequential search statements were counted only once. A hit was defined as a search that retrieved an item-level display, while searches that never retrieved an item-level display were called zero hits. Some of the searches were replicated. Overall, 54.2 percent of the searches retrieved zero hits. Subject searching had the highest zero-hit rate (62 percent), followed by title (47.9 percent) and author (42.3 percent) searching. Entering an author's first name first caused 15.2 percent of the author searches to fail. Entering initial articles during title searches caused 13.6 percent of the title searches to fail. Hunter states that visually analyzing transaction logs is an excellent and cost-effective way for reference librarians to determine how the online catalog is being used. (revised by Tom Peters)

Ingwersen, Peter. 1982. Search procedures in the library—analyzed from the cognitive point of view. *Journal of Documentation* 38: 165–191.

Ingwersen describes a research project focusing on the cognitive aspects of information-retrieval processes in public libraries, especially the user-librarian negotiation process, the librarian's search processes (both thought processes and behavior patterns), and the user's interaction with the organization of documents. This research draws on theories from cognitive science and cognitive psychology.

He notes that the reference librarian faces a very complicated task of transforming user questions and concepts into the underlying needs, then directing and restructuring those needs to fit the organization of documents or the organization of the information within the documents. Data were collected between 1976 and 1980 by audio recordings (the "think aloud" technique). Thirteen librarians and five users served as subjects. The think aloud method minimizes the danger of confusing past and present states of knowledge. The audio-taped data were supplemented by observation of the subjects' behavior and self-confrontation (i.e., adding comments while the audio recording is being replayed). Ingwersen was interested in how the user's knowledge structures coped with the structures of the system. The functions of open and closed questions are examined. Ingwersen concludes that matching the knowledge structures of user and librarian is a kind of learning process. (revised by Tom Peters)

Isenstein, Laura J. 1991. On the road to STARdom: Improving reference accuracy. *Illinois Libraries* 73: 146–151.

Isenstein describes a staffwide reference accuracy training program at the Baltimore County Public Library (BCPL). The program known as STARS (Staff Trained for Accurate Reference Service) was built upon a 1986 Maryland Division of Library Development and Services workshop in reference accuracy, which raised reference accuracy in numerous Maryland libraries from an average of 55 percent in 1983 to 77 percent in 1986. This article focuses on how the BCPL trained their staff to use the new system, particularly the methods of peer coaching and developing technical feedback skills. A 1987 series of follow-up workshops lasted five days and concentrated on the behavioral process of reference (setting the tone, getting the facts, giving the information, and follow-up); technical feedback (the process of giving regular feedback to reference librarians on their degree of conformance with model reference behaviors); and the importance of using model reference behaviors (clarifying, paraphrasing, probing, verifying, and asking follow-up questions). Asking follow-up questions was shown to increase reference accuracy to 94 to 98 percent. In 1988 the BCPL reduced the five-day workshops to one and one-half days and systematically introduced the program to several hundred staff members. Management support was critical for program success. In 1991 the BCPL also incorporated staff performance measures which evaluated staff partially on the degree of their utilization of the model reference behaviors, with a goal of 80-percent utilization. (revised by Frank Elliott and Paula Contreras)

Kantor, Paul B. 1980. Analyzing the availability of reference services. In *Library effectiveness: A state of the art: Proceedings of the ALA preconference on library effectiveness,* ed. Neal Kaske, 131–149. Chicago: American Library Association.

> This contributed chapter describes the observational and self-reported data collected from sixteen libraries on a number of factors related to the availability and effectiveness of library reference services. The observed factors were the number of patrons awaiting service, the number of reference personnel free to serve, the number of personnel engaged in providing service, and the number of personnel otherwise engaged. Some very useful and well-known measures were derived from these data, including the frustration factor (the probability that someone is available to serve) and the nuisance factor (the ratio of waiting time to time spent receiving help). There is also a detailed analysis and discussion of the five causal factors for reference failure (communication, knowledge, collection, source, patron). Finally, there is a thought-provoking chart of the probability of all these causal factors being successfully surmounted in each of the libraries studied. This article contains many ideas and methods that could be used today. It would be especially fascinating to revise and expand the ideas of availability, behavior outcomes, and the causal factors contributing to reference failure in light of the technological advances of the last twenty years. This article contains the theoretical basis for many more useful studies in the electronic reference environment. (revised by Frank Elliott)

Kantor, Paul B. 1981. Quantitative evaluation of the reference process. *RQ* 21: 43–52.

> Kantor analyzed the success of the reference process using self-reported data from librarians at sixteen libraries. Information from more than two thousand questions was gathered using a tally sheet to record behavior outcomes for each reference question as well as causal outcomes. The behavioral outcomes included: try again, refer elsewhere, patron gave up, and patron appears satisfied. The causal outcomes included: question not understood, and we don't

have the source. While there are difficulties in data collection using self-reported data, the author used the approach because only the librarian has specific information about both the causes of failure and the behavioral outcomes. The success rate in the study was 73 percent. Kantor concluded that in studies of reference success, it is important to separate outcomes from causal factors because, for example, an outcome such as "patron gave up" can have many different causes, including collection failure, librarian failure, or a question inappropriate for the library. (revised by Susan Clark)

King, Geraldine. 1982. Try it—you'll like it: A comprehensive management information system for reference service. *Reference Librarian,* no. 3: 71–78.

King describes a method of detailed data-gathering for reference questions. She developed a reference transaction slip to be filled out for every reference question. The date, time, author/title, and the user's question were recorded, along with the sources checked to answer the question and the disposition or solution to the question. As associate director of a public library, King used the transaction slips for training and evaluating reference librarians as well as for evaluating library resources for collection development. Data from the slips also was used to analyze workload. The author notes that at first reference librarians objected to using the slips, but once they used them, they did not want to stop. Analysis of the slips provided data on reference success as well as known item versus subject searches, gaps in library resources, student versus adult requests, and phone versus in-person questions. (revised by Susan Clark)

Moore, Carolyn M., and Linda Mielke. 1986. Taking the measure: Applying reference outputs to collection development. *Public Libraries* 25: 108–110.

The purpose of this study was to evaluate the reference collection and improve collection development and service at a public library. The study used four reference measures from *Output Measures for Public Libraries* (ALA, 1982): turnover rate of reference materials, in-library use of reference materials, reference question fill rate, and reference transactions per capita. Data were gathered by Dewey category in order to identify areas of the collection needing development. The authors concluded that the output measures were useful monitors of the reference collection and service. (revised by Susan Clark)

Morgan, Linda. 1980. Patron preference in reference service points. *RQ* 19: 373–375.

> Morgan examined the effect of two different heights of reference desks on patrons' choice of whom to approach with a reference question. Reference interactions in two libraries at the University of Houston were observed. Both libraries had a high counter and a low desk. When two staff members were on duty at the general reference desk, and both were free, 72 percent of patrons preferred to ask the person at the high counter. In both locations, a number of patrons chose to wait for the staff person at the counter even if the person at the low desk was free. The author concluded that the reference librarians' efforts to be research consultants and not work at counters may have a negative effect on patrons' willingness to ask questions. (revised by Susan Clark)

* Nardi, Bonnie, and Vicki O'Day. 1996. Intelligent agents: What we learned at the library. *Libri* 46: 59–88.

> A rarity in library literature, this article provides an outsider's perspective on the way reference librarians interact with patrons. In a quest to develop effective software agents, the authors observed human agents (librarians) in the process of providing expert service. Nardi and O'Day conducted ethnographic studies (through observation and interviews) in two corporate libraries, at Apple and Hewlett-Packard, with the goal of determining what reference librarians do every day. They concluded that librarians are exemplary agents because of the way they communicate with patrons, and because of their technical competence in performing searches. While the authors are able to come up with desirable attributes for software agents based on their study, they also find that there are a number of elements of information retrieval that software agents will not be able to replicate. Common types of reference searches (monitoring, planned, and exploratory) are outlined, and the term "intelligent software agent" is defined, as well as requirements for personalizing task performance in the fashion of librarians. (annotated by Paula Contreras)

* Paskoff, Beth M. 1991. Accuracy of telephone reference service in health sciences libraries. *Bulletin of the Medical Library Association* 79: 182–188.

> Six factual reference questions were unobtrusively telephoned to 51 academic and hospital health-science libraries in the United

States. The six questions were pretested in five different libraries. Paskoff asserts that the quality of reference services can be evaluated by asking reference questions and evaluating the responses received. The author notes how important it is that the questions used in unobtrusive assessment projects be typical of the reference questions actually received by the reference service units being assessed. The author and a female graduate student made the phone calls. The use of same-gender callers reduced the probability of gender bias by the reference service units being studied. The majority of the responses (63.4 percent) were accurate. A follow-up survey of the 51 libraries was undertaken to learn more about the explanations health sciences librarians offer about the accuracy or inaccuracy of their telephone reference services. Paskoff discerned a correlation between the number of accurate answers provided and the presence of at least one staff member with a master's degree in library and information science. This article is a synopsis of Paskoff's doctoral dissertation. (annotated by Tom Peters)

Peters, Thomas A. 1989. When smart people fail: An analysis of the transaction log of an online public access catalog. *Journal of Academic Librarianship* 15: 267–273.

Peters reports on both the methodology and results of a transaction log analysis of the online public access catalog at the University of Missouri at Kansas City from October 1987 through February 1988. The study tested the viability of using a transaction log as a source for everyday information in an academic library. It found the transaction log could be an excellent source of information to aid in planning for bibliographic instruction, collection development, and online catalog instruction. Transaction logs supplement survey data about attitudes and behaviors with objective information which is not as susceptible to response bias as survey data. One of the major problems in using transaction logs is the lack of a standardized way of gathering, comparing, and reporting the results. Although this problem is not solved, a methodology for both coding data and reporting results was developed. The three specific goals of the study were to determine failure rates, to study usage patterns, and to investigate the causes of patron failure. Many patrons tended to use poor, inefficient, high-recall searches rather than working to refine searches and increase search precision. Peters points out the unique value of transaction logs and argues that they should be more generally accepted and widely used. (revised by Frank Elliott)

* Quinn, Brian. 1994. Beyond efficacy: The exemplar librarian as a new approach to reference evaluation. *Illinois Libraries* 76: 163–173.

Quinn's goal was to develop a holistic approach to evaluating reference service by studying the work of exemplary reference librarians. Quinn suggests that, if we want to know the components of good or great reference service, we need to study the activities of exemplary reference librarians. Librarians were queried via the LibRef, LibAdmin, and University of Illinois networks with paper questionnaires sent to reference staff members at two local public libraries. The sole question was posed in a casual, unstructured form. Quinn was looking for specific, observable behaviors that could be used as evaluation standards. He wanted to minimize responses that focused on character traits and personality variables. Content analysis (a method of analyzing the content of documents and other forms of communication in a methodical and quantitative manner) was used to analyze the responses. Twenty-two classification categories were established, and fifty-two responses were received. Command of reference resources was mentioned most often as a behavioral trait of exemplary reference librarians ($n = 22$), followed by respect for the patron and the question ($n = 15$), and approachability ($n = 13$). Quinn concludes that great reference librarianship is neither magical nor mystical. It can be learned, and is not a cluster of innate abilities. Attitude and interpersonal skills are as important as information-retrieval skills. (annotated by Tom Peters)

* Ricks, Thomas W., Sheri Orth, and Jonathan Buckley. 1991. Finding the real information need: An evaluation of reference negotiation skills. *Public Libraries* 30: 159–164.

Negotiating the real information need is the underlying basis of quality reference service. The authors sought to determine how frequently reference questions were negotiated in order to identify the specific and complete information need; to determine how frequently these fully negotiated questions were answered correctly; and to determine what verbal and nonverbal communication skills contributed to correct answers. Nine reference librarians in the Orem (Utah) Public Library were tested unobtrusively by eighteen proxy patrons to determine their use of verbal and nonverbal skills and their ability to negotiate the real information need. Twenty questions were developed and asked three times for a total of sixty reference transactions over a four-month period. Each question had three levels. Level one introduced a broad question, and level two provided additional information. At level three, librarians needed to demonstrate appropriate negotiation skills to elicit the specific and complete information need. Questions that reached level three produced the highest percentage of correct answers (78.1 percent). Reference questions answered at level one received only incorrect or no answers. Although nonverbal skills were used 90 percent of the time, these communication skills were not indicative of receiving correct answers. Rather, the use of verbal negotiation skills to identify the real information need led to correct answers. The use of open questions and follow-up were most significant (78.6 and 70 percent, respectively) in receiving correct answers. (annotated by Mary Parker)

Rodger, Eleanor Jo, and Jane Goodwin. 1987. To see ourselves as others see us: A cooperative do-it-yourself reference accuracy study. *Reference Librarian,* no. 18: 135–147.

The purpose of this study was to unobtrusively measure the accuracy of answers provided through a telephone reference service at a multibranch public library system. Staff from nearby libraries in the system acted as proxy reference patrons. Each participating branch was asked twenty-five prepared questions: fifteen ready-reference questions, five in-system referrals, and five complex questions requiring negotiation. The data analysis revealed that although the ready-reference questions were answered accurately to a large extent, the library staff was less successful with the system-referral and negotiated questions. The results of this study aided management in its staff-training decisions. An academic library with a substantial telephone service could also benefit from such a study. (revised by Laura Dale Bischof)

* Ross, Catherine Sheldrick, and Patricia Dewdney. 1994. Best practices: An analysis of the best (and worst) in fifty-two public library reference transactions. *Public Libraries* 33: 261–266.

Since 1982, students in an introductory course in reference service at the Graduate School of Library and Information Science at the

University of Western Ontario have completed an assignment designed to help them understand what it is like to be the recipient rather than the provider of reference services. This unobtrusive study results from that assignment. Fifty-two students visited public libraries and asked a question of their own choosing. Each completed a questionnaire evaluating the experience as a user of public library reference services. The focus was on observing verbal and nonverbal communication skills and assessing the correctness of the answer provided. Only 54 percent of the students expressed a satisfactory experience and a willingness to return to the same librarian with another question. This is consistent with other studies. Twelve common communication barriers were identified. Training in five specific skills must be provided to reference staff: use of welcoming body language, use of open-ended questions, volunteering help, monitoring the referral, and use of follow-up. (annotated by Mary Parker)

Ross, Johanna. 1983. Observations of browsing behavior in an academic library. *College & Research Libraries* 44: 269–276.

Ross used unobtrusive observation to study user browsing activity at the Physical Sciences Library at the University of California, Davis. Browsing was defined as any examination of books at the shelves. Browsing intensity was measured by recording the number of books removed and replaced, and the time spent browsing. Items taken out of the stacks area were not counted in this browsing study, because they could be counted as circulations or refiles. Net browsing was defined as the number of books replaced. Random observations, in terms of both time and place, were used to collect the data. Forty intervals of 15 minutes each were selected for each week of a 13-week period, for a total of 520 intervals. Patrons were not informed that browsing behavior at the shelf was being studied. Only 98 observation periods failed to turn up a browsing patron, resulting in 422 useful intervals. The QA and QD Library of Congress call number ranges received the largest percentages of the total observed browsing activity. The mean number of books removed was 3.37, with a standard deviation of 2.72. The mean number of books replaced was 2.26. Over half of the observed browsers removed two books or less, but nearly 25 percent inspected five or more books, and approximately 4 percent removed ten or more books. The mean time browsers spent at the shelves was 6.94 minutes. Approximately 20 percent of the observed browsing sessions lasted at least 15 minutes. (revised by Tom Peters)

* Roy, Loriene. 1995. Reference accuracy. *Reference Librarian,* nos. 49–50: 217–227.

Roy explores qualitative and quantitative measurements for correctness and accuracy in the question-answering component of reference service. Roy reviews earlier studies in order to discuss the factors affecting accuracy in both academic and public library settings, including professional preparation and education, inviting patrons to provide feedback, projection of attitudes, the reference setting, local policies, the reference collection, and how patrons used their time with reference librarians. Roy then challenges the use of accuracy as a measure of success in reference question negotiation by identifying five underlying assumptions: (1) that librarians should continue to provide answers to reference questions; (2) that accuracy can be determined and error detected; (3) that another person can understand the patron's information need; (4) that librarians are responsible for improving the accuracy rate; and (5) that patrons are concerned with accuracy issues. In Roy's experience, some patrons who were aware of inadequacy in the librarian's answers still reported satisfaction based on the usefulness of answers rather than on their accuracy. Roy recommends using accuracy as one step toward diagnosing improvements in reference service. (annotated by Patricia L. Gregory)

* Solomon, Paul. 1997. Conversation in information seeking contexts: A test of an analytical framework. *Library and Information Science Research* 19: 217–248.

In this article, Solomon subjects the reference interview to linguistic and sociolinguistic analysis. Linguistic behavior in Restricted Conversational Domains (as opposed to everyday conversation) is shown to display distinct characteristics, and is viewed in relation to conceptualizations of vocabulary, cohesion mechanisms, coherence mechanisms, turn taking, turn allocation, overlaps, conversational gaps, openings, closings, frame allocation, repairs, role specification, and other features. Definitions and descriptions of each are provided, and are examined in the context of public library and school library reference interviews. Findings from this study are suggested to have value in the training and evaluation of information specialists, as well as in system design and in human-computer dialogues. (annotated by Paula Contreras)

Spencer, Carol C. 1980. Random time sampling. *Bulletin of the Medical Library Association* 68: 53–57.

A work-sampling study was performed at the National Library of Medicine, where staff were given a pocket-sized random alarm mechanism and were asked to record on a form categories of reference questions engaged in when the alarm sounded. Approximately forty observations per day were obtained for two months, covering a total of 1,566 working hours. The number of alarms involving verification questions, for example, was divided by the total number of alarms to obtain the percentage of time the staff worked on verification questions. This percentage was then multiplied by the total number of hours worked (1.566) to obtain the number of estimated hours spent working on verification. This method was used to determine the costs per question for different types of questions. The use of beepers to collect a random sample of data about reference service activity worked well. (revised by Tom Peters)

Van House, Nancy A., and Thomas Childers. 1984. Unobtrusive evaluation of a reference referral network: The California experience. *Library and Information Science Research* 6: 305–319.

Van House and Childers discuss the performance of California's reference referral network using unobtrusive means. Using transcripts of actual questions collected from one hundred sites, a panel of judges reviewed and evaluated the responses for correctness. While the local libraries typically found complete and mostly correct answers only half of the time, the network components found complete and mostly correct answers about 79 percent of the time. Once a question was referred to the network as a whole, the probability was 92 percent that an answer to the question would be found that was mostly correct or better. This study differs from other unobtrusive studies because it used an actual sampling of reference questions answered by the libraries and network components being examined. (revised by John Mess)

* Welch, Jeanie M., Lynn A. Cauble, and Lara B. Little. 1997. Automated reshelving statistics as a tool in reference collection management. *Reference Services Review: RSR* 25 (3/4): 79–85.

The authors reviewed previous studies that measured the usage of reference collections. The focus was using reshelving as the method to measure use. Tally sheets and spine marking are two common techniques in reshelving studies. Both of these manual methods of data collection have disadvantages, however. Automation provides a new tool to evaluate collections via circulation and usage studies. This study recorded the item numbers on the bar codes of all re-shelved reference volumes as they were reshelved. The call numbers of items without bar codes were recorded manually. Data were entered into a spreadsheet software program; data were recorded for item numbers, the number of times each volume was reshelved, the call number of the item, and the title of the volume. Statistics were presented by lists of titles arranged by call number and graphs arranged by Library of Congress classification. The results of the study were used for purchasing, bindery, and weeding decisions. (annotated by Mary Parker)

* Whittaker, Kenneth. 1990. Unobtrusive testing of reference inquiry work. *Library Review* 39 (6): 50–54.

Whittaker reviews the history and development of unobtrusive reference-assessment research at the Manchester Polytechnic's Department of Library and Information Studies. Whittaker asserts that the answering of specific reference queries has always been an important part of the services offered by all kinds of libraries. The unobtrusive testing technique has proven to be a valid test measure, even though the results are sometimes embarrassing to the library profession. He compares the ethical dilemmas of library school researchers with the ethical challenges of library managers conducting unobtrusive assessment of the quality of reference service. Whittaker concludes that half-right reference is true of British libraries, as well as of North American ones. Improving the communication skills of reference service providers is the best way of improving question-answering performance. Whittaker notes that if unobtrusive testing were undertaken on other areas of library service, such as online database searching, bibliographic instruction, and outreach services, no doubt we would find that the quality of these services also leaves something to be desired. (annotated by Tom Peters)

Woodard, Beth S. 1989. The effectiveness of an information desk staffed by graduate students and nonprofessionals. *College & Research Libraries* 50: 455–467.

> Woodard designed an unobtrusive test of information desk service when provided by graduate assistants and nonprofessionals in an academic library. The test contained five categories of questions: (1) bibliographic (i.e., whether the library owned a particular book or journal with a known title or author); (2) research guidance (how to find information on a particular subject); (3) procedural or instructional (request for information on how to use a library source); (4) ready reference (request for brief factual information); and (5) directional (locations of library facilities, collections, or staff). The questions used in testing were actual questions recorded during 1986 at the University of Illinois, Urbana-Champaign. The questions were asked only in person, never over the telephone. Of those questions capable of being answered at the information desk, the highest success levels by question type were for directional and procedural questions. The findings of Murfin and Bunge are supported by Woodard's study, which indicates that more accurate answers and referrals are provided when staff members are available for consultation. (revised by Tom Peters)

See also the following annotations in the section on chapter 7 of part IV: Christensen et al. (1989), Radford (1998), Von Seggern (1989).

CHAPTER 6
FOCUS GROUPS AND INTERVIEWS

* Childers, Thomas A. 1997. Using public library reference collections and staff. *Library Quarterly* 67: 155–173.

> Three studies were conducted to explore library users' success in non-mediated and mediated use of printed reference materials in public libraries. Fifty-seven interviews were conducted with primarily Anglo users at the main branch of the Santa Monica Public Library; forty-four interviews were conducted with Hispanic users at the Fullerton Public Library, and thirty-six interviews were conducted with Vietnamese users at the Linda Vista branch of the San Diego Public Library. The interview instrument is not reproduced in this article, but eleven questions are listed. Some of the ques-

tions were: Did you find the answer or any part of the answer? Did you seek help in the search? If you didn't ask for staff help, why not? How complete was the information found? How useful is the information likely to be? The results indicated that most users from all three ethnic groups felt that their unmediated and mediated reference use was successful. There were indications, however, that additional staff intervention could lead to better search results. (annotated by Susan Clark)

Dervin, Brenda. 1992. From the mind's eye of the user: The sense-making qualitative-quantitative methodology. In *Qualitative research in information management,* ed. Jack D. Glazier and Ronald D. Powell, 61–84. Englewood, Colo.: Libraries Unlimited.

Dervin tries to turn some of the assumptions underlying reference evaluation on their head, noting that we must study the information-seeking process from the viewpoint of the user, not the observer. Sense-making research, pioneered by Dervin, is defined as "a programmatic research effort specifically focused on developing alternative approaches to the study of human use of information and information systems." The rationale and theoretical foundations of the approach are discussed, and its methodology is illustrated with diagrams. Users' information needs are viewed in context, as a three-sided triangle—situation, gap, and use/help—where users try to overcome barriers in their pursuit of information. Seeing information needs in this way should help librarians design effective user evaluations, whether in framing questions or in collecting and analyzing data. Six "exemplar" studies show sense-making in action. One shows respondents focusing on one step of their information-seeking process, while another shows how users perceive the messages conveyed in instruction manuals. Central to all these studies is the research interview. Taken together, they show that "the ways in which people see their gaps will be related to the ways in which people try to bridge them and not to characteristics of persons independent of their gaps." The sense-making approach is generalizable to all types of libraries. (revised by Jim Stemper)

Goldhor, Herbert. 1979. The patrons' side of public library reference questions. *Public Library Quarterly* 1: 35–49.

The purpose of the study outlined here was to gather information about reference interactions from the patrons' point of view. One hundred telephone reference patrons from the Urbana Free Library participated in the study by answering a series of questions after the completion of the call. The survey focused on the origin of the reference question, how the patron used the information provided, satisfaction with the answer, and perception of the librarian's role. Since reference staff only asked patrons to participate when time and the situation allowed, this study serves more as a trial than as an empirical random-sample investigation. Ninety-one percent of the patrons used the information they received from the library, and approximately 95 percent were satisfied with the answer. The largest percentage of the questions was personal in nature, and the second-largest percentage was job-related, followed by school-related questions and curiosity. (revised by Laura Dale Bischof)

Hatchard, Desmond B., and Phyllis Toy. 1986. The psychological barriers between library users and library staff—an exploratory investigation. *Australian Academic and Research Libraries* 17 (2): 63–69.

Hatchard and Toy report on an exploratory study that sought to identify the psychological barriers between college students (including a smaller sample of academic staff) and library staff. Six academic and research libraries participated in the study. A total of ninety-four students and twenty academic staff were interviewed using a semi-structured interview method, which was created by representatives from the six participating institutions. A trained interviewer conducted the interviews. The findings suggest that student personality traits affect how students feel about asking for reference assistance. (revised by Tom Peters)

* Massey-Burzio, Virginia. 1998. From the other side of the reference desk: A focus group study. *Journal of Academic Librarianship* 24: 208–215.

The author assesses the quality and effectiveness of reference service, emphasizing patron needs and preferences. This focus group study conducted at Johns Hopkins University was designed to elicit information from patrons about how they were dealing with the rapidly changing technological environment. Six focus groups were conducted over a twelve-month period, with groups divided by type: undergraduates, graduate students, and faculty. Group size ranged from four to ten, with a total of thirty-eight participants. The focus group sessions were audiotaped. The confidentiality of comments was assured. Massey-Burzio notes that focus groups are a good way to gain information about the experiences, thoughts, concerns, and values of library users. Focus group discussions can elicit information on non-threatening topics (e.g., information seeking) and explore unanticipated issues as they arise. Several themes emerged from the sessions. Many users feel uncomfortable asking questions, and most feel they know how to find information on their own. Participants viewed the paraprofessionals as unfriendly and unhelpful. Most users were not interested in taking a class on how to use a library and find information. They wanted single-sheet explanations of a few key points and hints. Massey-Burzio concluded that focus groups are also good public relations for the library. (annotated by Tom Peters)

* Meltzer, Ellen, Patricia Maughan, and Thomas K. Fry. 1995. Undergraduate in focus: Can student input lead to new directions in planning undergraduate services? *Library Trends* 44: 400–422.

The authors combined focus groups and interviews to help make decisions on strategic planning for the University of California library system. The main methodology discussed is focus groups. The authors provide historical information on focus groups, along with why it is important to use focus groups for customer input. The article also strives to give readers guidelines on how to get started choosing questions that will produce the most information. The focus group and interview data were examined and analyzed, and the authors explain how the information was used to make changes at their library system. The methodologies (focus groups and interviews) were not used to examine reference service, but the article is a valuable background resource from which to learn more about focus groups. The qualitative research can be duplicated at both public and academic libraries. (annotated by Elaina Norlin)

* Morgan, David L. and Richard A. Krueger, eds. 1998. *The focus group kit*. 6 vols. Thousand Oaks, Calif.: Sage.

Vol. 1. *The focus group guidebook,* David L. Morgan. Vol. 2. *Planning focus groups,* David L. Morgan. Vol. 3. *Developing questions for focus groups,* Richard A. Krueger. Vol. 4. *Moderating focus groups,* Richard A. Krueger. Vol. 5. *Involving community members in focus groups,* Richard A. Krueger, Jean A. King. Vol. 6. *Analyzing and reporting focus group results,* Richard A. Krueger.

This six-volume set provides a guide for both novices and experts on focus group interviewing. The guide provides an overview of the basic issues and in-depth treatments of planning and conducting an actual study utilizing focus groups. The volumes include essential checklists, ideas, examples, and other practical tips. This set should be consulted by anyone planning to use focus groups. (annotated by Jo Bell Whitlatch)

* Mullaly-Quijas, Peggy, Deborah H. Ward, and Nancy Woelfl. 1994. Using focus groups to discover health professionals' information needs: A regional marketing study. *Bulletin of the Medical Library Association* 82: 305–311.

The authors begin the article by providing background information about focus groups, why they are important, and the benefits of using focus groups in library assessment. They also explain how to conduct a study utilizing focus groups from start to finish. The focus group sessions allowed the librarians to gather more in-depth information on potential and current clients. From this information, the authors explain how they analyzed the results to make changes within their particular library. Although they contracted a marketing firm to moderate and analyze the results, they do explain the steps one would need to take to get this project off the ground. This comprehensive, well-researched article is applicable to public, special, and academic library settings. (annotated by Elaina Norlin)

* Radford, Marie Louise. 1996. Communication theory applied to the reference encounter: An analysis of critical incidents. *Library Quarterly* 66: 123–137.

Radford applies the relational communication-centered approach to the interpersonal dynamics between librarian and user. She examines reference encounters to determine users' perceptions of the success or failure of particular library experiences in three diverse academic libraries. Using John Flanagan's critical incident technique, Radford interviewed 9 librarians and 27 users for 10 to 15 minutes each on audiotape. Informants were asked to recall successful and unsuccessful transactions, and these incidents were sorted into content-oriented or relational-oriented statements. Forty-seven incidents were collected, and the transcripts were further analyzed for underlying relational and content themes based on

Watzlawick, Beavin, and Jackson's relational theory. Separate analyses were done for librarians and users on the critical incident themes of attitude, information, knowledge base, and relationship quality, with the theme of approachability added for users. Both librarians and users ranked attitude as the most important factor, but with other themes, librarians ranked information factors higher, while users rated relational categories higher. Radford concludes that librarians need to become more sensitive to nonverbal behavioral cues exhibited by themselves and by users, and that future research should emphasize relational theory. (annotated by Patricia L. Gregory)

* Radford, Marie Louise. 1999. *The reference encounter: Interpersonal communication in the academic library.* Chicago: Association of College & Research Libraries, American Library Association.

Radford challenges the assumption that the goal of reference service has remained constant—to answer questions. Another important goal is to build positive relationships with library users. Her research was driven by the conviction that a full understanding and appreciation of the interpersonal communication process between reference librarian and user is vital to a successful reference encounter. Interpersonal communication has two basic dimensions. The content-oriented dimension is the report aspect of the message, i.e., what is being said. The relational dimension is the command aspect of a message, i.e., how the message is said, and how it is received. In her study Radford sought to have users themselves define effective reference service. Chapter 4 of her book describes the methodology for site and subject selection, the data-collection instruments and techniques, and the three data-analysis methods used: (1) development of a category scheme, reflecting the relational and content dimensions of the librarian-user interaction; (2) examination of critical incidents (where interviewees recall and describe positive and negative interactions); and (3) comparison of the user's and librarian's paired perceptions of the interaction. The research reported here involved in-depth interviews following 27 academic library reference interactions. The nine participating librarians were also interviewed prior to their reference interactions. Radford seems to concur with Dervin that communication theory, rather than information theory, is more important for librarianship. (annotated by Tom Peters)

ANNOTATED BIBLIOGRAPHY

* Rose, Pamela M., Kristin Stoklosa, and Sharon A. Gray. 1998. A focus group approach to assessing technostress at the reference desk. *Reference & User Services Quarterly* 37: 311–317.

The authors conducted focus groups with teams of reference providers at the Health Sciences Library of the State University of New York at Buffalo who seemed to be experiencing high levels of strain and anxiety. The authors hypothesized that the increased level of anxiety was correlated with the increase in end-user access to electronic resources. Eight female librarians (whose primary responsibilities were not in reference) and library science students participated. The authors explain why the focus group approach was chosen over other data collection methods. The researchers felt the focus group situation would elicit more discussion than individual interviews and that the discussion would bring out more information. Respondents associated telephone reference interactions with feelings of incompleteness, anxiety, and overwork. The respondents agreed that patrons in a highly technological information environment generally are demanding, have unrealistic expectations of computerized information-retrieval systems, and do not use critical thinking skills. The four major causes of stress at the reference desk for reference providers were technology, patrons, environmental factors, and staffing limitations. An analysis of the information gathered during the focus group resulted in a set of eleven recommendations meant to decrease anxiety among the reference desk staff. A brief discussion of the implementation of these recommendations is given. (annotated by Tom Peters and Jeanette Moore Piquet)

Swope, Mary Jane, and Jeffrey Katzer. 1972. Silent majority: Why don't they ask questions? *RQ* 12: 161–166.

The majority of reference assessment studies focus on the questions answered by the librarians. This study, in contrast, measures reference service not given, using interviews with patrons who did not ask for assistance at the reference desk. Patrons were interviewed in non-reference locations, such as by the card catalog, in the reference area, and in the open stacks. They were asked if they needed assistance and if they would ask for help from the reference librarian. Forty-one percent of those interviewed did need help, but did not plan to ask for help from librarians. Three causes for this were cited: previous dissatisfaction with the librarian, a feeling that the question was too simple, or fear of interrupting the librarian. The results of this study suggest that librarians are not serving their entire user population. Library educators and practicing librarians need further training in customer service and personal (as well as patron) nonverbal communication issues. (revised by Lorrie Knight)

CHAPTER 7
CASE STUDIES

* Aluri, Rao. 1993. Improving reference service: The case for using a continuous quality improvement method. *RQ* 33: 220–236.

Using Deming's total quality management principles and an extensive review of reference evaluation studies, Aluri identifies three main problems with reference assessment: using outside evaluators, which puts librarians in a "win-lose" situation; one-shot evaluations; and lack of a systems perspective. Aluri recommends continuous evaluation to achieve "win-win" cooperation and improvements. A manufacturing analogy illustrates how quality control problems must be improved by starting with product design rather than with operators (i.e., reference librarians) at the end of the process. Library managers and reference librarians must understand overall administrative policies and procedures, and collect long-term data to identify the causes of poor-quality reference service. Besides collecting quantifiable data, reference librarians must identify key quality aspects to measure, preferably in an atmosphere that promotes the open exchange of ideas. Aluri advocates the use of checksheets, control charts, and Pareto charts to identify superficial problems, followed by cause-and-effect diagrams, obtrusive and unobtrusive methods, and normal and planted reference queries to locate the root causes of problems under standard categories such as environment, people, materials, machines, or evaluation method. Aluri sees reference librarians' goal as decreasing and eventually eliminating the number of missed opportunities to provide quality reference service by using the aforementioned tools, a long-term perspective, teamwork, and a systems view. (annotated by Patricia L. Gregory)

Arthur, Gwen. 1990. Peer coaching in a university reference department. *College & Research Libraries* 51: 367–373.

> In an effort to extend its staff development program, the Temple University reference department implemented a semester-long peer coaching program focused on reference skills and behavior. Findings from previous studies indicated that critical factors in the reference interview were not taught easily in traditional programs and workshops designed to keep staff aware of new tools. Findings from unobtrusive studies indicated that correct responses were strongly associated with staff behavior, question negotiation, and follow-up behaviors. Peer coaching includes: (1) selecting a coach one trusts, (2) creating a contract with objectives, (3) providing observation by coach and coachee, and (4) providing feedback not linked to job evaluation. This approach aimed to provide interactive, observable reinforcement; minimize specialized subject expertise; and impart behaviors shown to improve the quality of reference service. The program concentrated on the objective observation of behavior. The aim of the program was to provide objective feedback, not evaluation, of reference behavior. At the end of the semester, the reference staff evaluated the usefulness of the peer coaching program. Participants reported that being coached sensitized them to question negotiation and made them generally more aware of their interpersonal and communication styles. The observers reported that being able to observe other staff members in action was valuable and instructive. (revised by John Mess)

* Brown, Janet Dagenais. 1994. Using quality concepts to improve reference services. *College & Research Libraries* 55: 211–219.

> Brown outlines the Wichita State University library's attempt to apply lessons and techniques from the business movement for quality service and customer satisfaction. The business and organizational management literature suggested that quality service efforts must have four major components: a commitment to improve quality; involvement of employees in the improvement process; continuous improvement; and identifying customers and their needs—the first and most important step toward improving service quality. The library undertook four projects. First, a problem log was developed to document the problems that patrons and staff encountered at the reference desk regarding materials, equipment, and services.

A wide variety of computers and new technologies led to patron and staff frustration The need for better signage and additional instructional handouts became evident. Second, a suggestion box was implemented to solicit feedback as well as to post responses. Third, a survey was conducted using the Reference Transaction Assessment Instrument from the Wisconsin-Ohio Reference Evaluation Program (WOREP). The results were compared with those of other libraries involved in WOREP. Results indicated that undergraduates often did not receive adequate assistance because the reference desk was busy. Finally, a Reference Automation Quality Circle was established to address issues surrounding technology overload. Recommendations from this team resulted in student assistants being hired to staff a computer assistance desk. (annotated by Razia Nanji)

Christensen, John O., et al. 1989. An evaluation of reference desk service. *College & Research Libraries* 50: 468–483.

A trend in academic libraries is to staff reference desks with library assistants and students. This study tested how effective student workers were while serving at reference desks staffed primarily by library departmental assistants and students. Fifteen library staff acted as proxy patrons and asked a total of seventy-five questions prepared to test accuracy, reference negotiation, referral, and bibliographic skills. The student reference assistants answered only 36 percent of the questions correctly. This outcome, along with the results of an opinion survey of library assistants, subject specialists, and students, led to recommendations for service standards, additional training, and greater involvement by subject specialists in reference services. (revised by Laura Dale Bischof)

* Davenport, Elisabeth, Rob Procter, and Ana Goldenberg. 1997. Distributed expertise: Remote reference service on a metropolitan area network. *Electronic Library* 15: 271–278.

The authors explored the possibilities and typologies of collaborative academic reference service in a digital library environment. Three reference service programs and the University of Edinburgh, Heriot-Watt University, and Napier University were connected with library users. The prototype system can be found at www.remote. lib.ac.uk. The approach used was similar to NERD, the Newcastle

Electronic Reference Desk (www.ndl.ac.uk/library). One intent of the online reference development program was to support synchronous online reference consultations through the provision of various real-time conferencing tools, including text, audio, and video. The authors wanted to design the user interface so that it would improve users' judgments about when and where to seek various types of reference assistance. Game theory was used to evaluate the efficacy of different modes of interaction on the Web. For six months the researchers worked with reference librarians at the three institutions, end-users, and the EDINA user group—a United Kingdom-wide group of librarians evaluating the beta version of a dedicated BIOSIS interface. Data were gathered via interviews, diaries, videotapes of peer consultations among reference librarians, and direct observation. (annotated by Tom Peters)

Devore-Chew, Marynell, Brian Roberts, and Nathan Smith. 1988. The effects of reference librarians' nonverbal communications on the patrons' perceptions of the library, librarians, and themselves. *Library and Information Science Research* 10: 389–400.

The authors studied the impact of nonverbal communication on patrons' perceptions. Conducted at the Lee Library of Brigham Young University, the study included a convenience sample of 354 patrons (187 males and 167 females) who approached the reference desk during a series of randomly selected hours. Reference assistants were taught to perform one of a series of eight different combinations of the presence or absence of touch, forward lean, and smile arranged in a changing random order during a two-hour period divided into eight fifteen-minute segments. The first patron who approached the reference desk during each fifteen-minute time segment was chosen as the experimental subject. Each patron completing an interaction at the reference desk was subsequently asked a series of fifteen questions. The results of the study were analyzed through analysis of variance and multiple analysis of variance and tended to confirm the null hypothesis that there would be no relationship "between the nonverbal communications of librarians' touch, forward lean, smile, and patrons' perceptions of the library, librarians, and themselves." These results seem to contradict the findings of other studies which showed a significant impact for nonverbal communications. (revised by Frank Elliott)

* Dow, Ronald F. 1998. Using assessment criteria to determine library quality. *Journal of Academic Librarianship* 24: 277–281.

> Dow notes that the assessment movement in higher education of the late 1980s has been joined by the accountability movement of the 1990s. Dow's purpose is to view academic libraries through the dual lenses of the assessment and accountability movements. He explains how the River Campus Libraries of the University of Rochester have created an assessment program that focuses on the educational impact of library services. The libraries used the American Association of Higher Education's "Principles of Good Practice for Assessing Student Learning" to establish the libraries' assessment strategy. Dow argues that libraries should look at their programs, rather than at their resource base, as a means of understanding their educational impact. Any assessment program should be fully integrated with the organizational and reward structure of the library. It should be directed at facilitating improvement in the program being assessed, rather than passively documenting performance from a distance. A central idea of this assessment initiative was that users must be given opportunities to share openly their ideas, concerns, and suggestions. The assessment exercises fell into four categories: surveys, focus groups, directed conversations, and longitudinal studies. By focusing assessment efforts on learners, learning, and the interpersonal aspects of campus life, the librarians were able to identify several opportunities for positive change. (annotated by Tom Peters)

Gothberg, Helen. 1976. Immediacy: A study of communication effect on the reference process. *Journal of Academic Librarianship* 2: 126–129.

> Gothberg examined the verbal and nonverbal communication of the reference librarian and its effect on question negotiation and user satisfaction. She applied Mehrabian's immediacy principle— that people draw close to things they value highly and withdraw from those they dislike—to examine the attitude of caring for the user through both verbal and nonverbal expression. Two librarians were trained to present both immediate (approaching) and non-immediate (distancing) behaviors and language cues. Both librarians presented both attitudes. Interactions with users were videotaped, and the users were asked to complete an evaluation. Judges

were used to evaluate the congruency of the attitude presentations by the librarians. The analysis showed that immediacy was significant in influencing users' satisfaction with the reference interview and their own comfort in asking questions. No significant interaction was found between the librarian's presented attitude (immediacy/non-immediacy) and the user's perception of how the answer was delivered. (revised by John Mess)

* Herman, Douglas. 1994. But does it work? Evaluating the Brandeis reference model. *Reference Services Review* 22 (4): 17–28.

Three different forms of assessment were used to study the effectiveness of the research consultation model at Brandeis University's Main Library: a librarian observation project, an information desk study, and a focus group evaluation. The goal was to evaluate tiered reference service in which an information desk is staffed by graduate students and a research consultation office is staffed by reference librarians. Each reference librarian observed seven one-hour sessions in the research consultation office over a four-month period. An unobtrusive telephone study was conducted in which one hundred questions were telephoned to the information desk by library staff members not known to the graduate student workers. The focus group evaluation consisted of seven focus groups of faculty, undergraduates, graduate students, and researchers. The results of the study were mostly positive, although inadequate referral of questions from the information desk to librarians indicated a need for additional training. (annotated by Susan Clark)

Kirby, Martha, and Naomi Miller. 1986. MEDLINE searching on Colleague: Reasons for failure or success of untrained end users. *Medical Reference Services Quarterly* 5: 17–34.

This study, conducted at the Medical College of Pennsylvania, compares the results of end-user biomedical professionals searching the MEDLINE and HEALTH databases on Colleague against experienced intermediaries performing the same search. End-users indicated that 60 percent of the time the intermediary's search was better than their own and contained more relevant citations. Most end-user searches that were judged successful were on topics with a simple search strategy that happened to work well. The majority of failures were due to search strategy problems. In conclusion, end-user searchers need to be warned against overconfidence in their search results. (revised by A. Craig Hawbaker)

Kuhlthau, Carol C. 1988. Developing a model of the library search process: Cognitive and affective aspects. *RQ* 28: 232–242.

Kuhlthau formulates a theory of the process of searching for information based on a study conducted in a large eastern suburban high school. Various theories of the search process are examined. An exploratory study was conducted using 26 high school seniors preparing research papers on a literary theme. The instruments and methods used were search logs, journals of feelings/thoughts/actions, flowcharts and time lines, observations, and short writings about topics. Six of the students agreed to be interviewed six times for 45-minute taped sessions. These data were used to develop a six-stage model of the search process: task initiation, topic selection, prefocus exploration, focus formulation, information collection, and search closure. (revised by Tom Peters)

Kuhlthau, Carol C., Betty J. Turock, Mary W. George, and Robert J. Belvin. 1990. Validating a model of the search process: A comparison of academic, public and school libraries. *Library and Information Science Research* 12: 5–31.

This research compares differences and similarities in the information-seeking process among a sample of public library adults, college undergraduate students, and high school students. Their perceptions, feelings, and experiences were studied during six phases of information seeking. During each phase data were collected using surveys, questionnaires, and flowcharts. While detailed results and tables are included, the general findings indicate that public library adults were significantly more confident at initiation of the search process. Undergraduate participants, however, were more confident at the closure stage than those in high school libraries. School library participants had significantly lower means in browsing and asking questions of librarians. The majority of participants expressed a preference for finding everything first and then reading, rather than the process-oriented approach. This research, which validates Kuhlthau's earlier studies done in high schools, opens a number of areas for further study. The authors suggest that reference librarians become sensitive to the stage of the process the user is in when a question is asked. (revised by A. Craig Hawbaker)

Markham, Marilyn, Keith H. Stirling, and Nathan M. Smith. 1983. Librarian self-disclosure and patron satisfaction in the reference interview. *RQ* 22: 369–374.

> The purpose of this study was to investigate whether self-disclosure on the part of librarians would promote patron satisfaction with the reference interview and a willingness to return again for reference aid. Two reference librarians and two student aides in an academic library were trained in self-disclosure. They each conducted sixteen reference interviews, eight with self-disclosure and eight without. A questionnaire was given to each patron after the reference interaction, and the results were analyzed. The results were mixed. Although self-disclosure had no significant effect on patron satisfaction or willingness to return, self-disclosure did seem to be effective in improving some aspects of the reference interview, such as communication with the patron. (revised by Susan Clark)

Mellon, Constance. 1986. Library anxiety: A grounded theory and its development. *College & Research Libraries* 47: 160–165.

> Mellon undertook a qualitative study to explore the feelings of undergraduate students about using an academic library for the first time for research. Samples of students' personal writing (in which the writer is talking on paper with no concern for audience, style, or the rules of grammar and spelling), collected in beginning composition courses over a two-year period, were analyzed for recurring themes. The constant comparative method of analysis was used. Mellon notes that qualitative studies focus on viewing experiences from the perspective of those involved. Unlike quantitative research, where the goal is to produce a replicable study in which different researchers working with the same methodology on the same data set would arrive at the same results, qualitative analysis strives to produce a unique theory that is grounded in the situation or event under study. The ethnographic techniques of anthropology and the qualitative methods of sociology can be applied to the study of library users. Mellon found that between 75 and 85 percent of the students in each composition class described their initial response to the library in terms of fear or anxiety. Feelings of being lost stemmed from four causes: the sheer size of the library, unfamiliarity with the location of things, ignorance about

how to begin, and ignorance about how to proceed. (revised by Tom Peters)

* Mendelsohn, Jennifer. 1997. Perspectives on quality of reference service in an academic library: A qualitative study. *RQ* 36: 544–557.

Mendelsohn conducted a qualitative study of the parameters of quality reference service in an academic library. The aim of qualitative research is to create a detailed understanding of a process by analyzing and describing complex human circumstances in context. In the study, two reference providers and two users were interviewed, and only experiences in the humanities and social sciences were analyzed. The meaning of "quality" as it applies to reference service is a key question. The analysis of the data focused on four factors (and their complex, dynamic interconnectedness) that may affect reference service: willingness, knowledge, morale, and time. For Mendelsohn, the primary function of academic library reference service is user independence or self-sufficiency. Quality reference service is a partnership between the librarian and user. Mendelsohn concluded that sufficient time and good morale are two essential aspects of a quality reference environment. As factors in quality reference service, time and morale are largely affected by management decisions and practices. The quality circle has four cycles: knowledge enables willingness; willingness leads to assessment; assessment produces action; and action enables knowledge. Action (i.e., physical movement by the librarian away from the desk) was evident in every instance of quality reference service. (annotated by Tom Peters)

Michell, B. Gillian, and Roma M. Harris. 1987. Evaluating the reference interview: Some factors influencing patrons and professionals. *RQ* 27: 95–105.

The authors conducted a study of the differing assessments made by public librarians and public library patrons as they observed videotapes of reference interviews. The actors playing reference librarians on the videotape varied in the amount of warmth they exhibited toward patrons, and in their efforts toward inclusion (i.e., the process whereby the librarian instructs the user in the process of using reference tools). As the teaching aspect of the reference interview, inclusion has both interpersonal and professional dimensions. The study found that the librarian viewers were harsher judges of competence than the patron viewers. Both groups, however, gave high competency ratings to librarians who exhibited high levels of warmth toward patrons. Unexpectedly, female librarians assigned lower competency ratings than either their male colleagues or patrons of either sex. This research focused on the social aspects of the reference encounter. Three social stimuli were isolated and examined: nonverbal warmth, inclusion, and gender. The results suggest that, especially for female librarians, the teaching aspect of reference service is very important. (revised by Tom Peters)

* Nassar, Anne. 1997. An evaluation of the Brandeis model of reference service at a small academic library. *Reference Librarian,* no. 58: 163–176.

The author examines the use of the Brandeis Model of Reference Service at Utica College, a liberal arts college with 2,300 undergraduate students, to determine if it is a viable service alternative in libraries with smaller staff and patron populations. The Brandeis model involves offering tiered reference service. Directional and non-reference questions are handled by paraprofessionals or student assistants. More complex questions are referred to the librarians in a separate, less heavily trafficked location. Based on library staff interviews, student assistant surveys, and patron satisfaction surveys, the author concludes that the Brandeis model is not effective at Utica. This is primarily due to the inconsistent training and motivation of student assistants, and a relatively low volume of nonreference activity. It is suggested that the Brandeis model might be better suited to large academic libraries. (annotated by Eric Novotny)

* Olszak, Lydia Pearl. 1991. Mistakes and failures at the reference desk. *RQ* 31: 39–49.

Acknowledging the findings of research conducted by Crowley and Childers, that patrons asking questions of reference staff receive incorrect answers 50 percent of the time, Olszak examines the nature and the underlying causes of reference mistakes. Her research consisted of observing reference transactions at a large, southeastern undergraduate library over the course of a semester and conducting interviews with several members of the reference staff. The author used three questions to guide her research. First, what actions or behaviors constitute a mistake in the eyes of reference staff? Second, how do staff alert one another that a mistake is or was being made? Finally, can reference mistakes be categorized to fit Bosk's typology of occupational mistakes: technical errors, judgment errors, normative errors, and quasi-normative errors? Olszak also explored the hypothesis that accuracy is only one of the goals of the reference staff and can be overshadowed by competing goals, such as instructing the patron, or minimizing transaction time. The author concludes that a framework for occupational mistakes, such as the one Bosk provides, can help to explain how and why mistakes are made in the reference department. (annotated by Jacob Carlson)

* Pinkston, Jane. 1992. Assessment and accountability at Toledo-Lucas County Public Library. *Reference Librarian,* no. 38: 41–52.

Pinkston describes the methods and techniques that the Toledo-Lucas County Public Library employs to evaluate its services and resources, hold itself accountable, and position itself for success. User surveys measure satisfaction levels and point out more immediate needs of their clientele, such as parking issues. Use of the Wisconsin-Ohio Reference Evaluation Program resulted in the evaluation of successful reference behaviors and more customer-service training. Circulation and usage statistics point to parts of the collection in need of development or physical rearrangement. The same statistics can be used to justify additional staff or reallocation. The ongoing evaluation of staff training and continuing education should also not be overlooked. Marketing research in terms of public relations and advertising is necessary to convey the library's vital role to the community's decision-makers. The concepts addressed in this article are relevant to the success of all types of libraries. (annotated by A. Craig Hawbaker)

Puttapithakporn, Somporn. 1990. Interface design and user problems and errors: A case study of novice searchers. *RQ* 30: 195–204.

Puttapithakporn studied and categorized the problems novice users encounter when searching a basic reference database—the Silverplatter CD-ROM version of the ERIC database. Data were collected via direct observation, self-administered questionnaires, and selective informal interviews. Thirty-three students enrolled in an introductory information-science course at Indiana University served as subjects. The questionnaire was administered after the completion of the first search session. During the analysis of the data, the author began by categorizing errors (i.e., any action that does not bring a user closer to the goal stated for the task at hand) into two major types: syntactic and semantic. Syntactic errors occur when the system does not respond at all or gives an error message. Semantic errors occur when the syntax is correct, but does not bring the user closer to the goal. System-use errors and inefficiencies (excluding typographical errors) were further categorized into incomplete screens, menu selection problems, inability to interpret abbreviations, misunderstanding of system messages, inability to exploit the full capability of the system, and crowded help screens. Analysis of the questionnaire responses revealed that users were frustrated with the print capabilities and confused by the display format, especially the abbreviated field codes. Puttapithakporn shows how user-centered evaluation of a computerized reference tool can be a useful form of reference assessment. (revised by Tom Peters)

* Radford, Marie Louise. 1998. Approach or avoidance? The role of nonverbal communication in the academic library user's decision to initiate a reference encounter. *Library Trends* 46: 699–717.

Radford studied the role of nonverbal communication during reference service interactions at two New Jersey academic libraries. She hypothesized that the nonverbal behavior exhibited by the librarian is related to the user's decision to approach. Data were collected via 37 hours of unobtrusive observation, and by interviewing 155 users who approached 34 librarian volunteers. The librarians, providing reference service in teams of two, did not know the specific design of the study. Ninety percent of the users were students. A content analysis of the data revealed five categories indicated by users as being critical in their decision to approach one librarian over another: initiation (explicit actions by librarians to initiate an encounter), availability (characterized by the librarian's open, yet passive, stance), familiarity (based on previous interaction with the chosen librarian), proximity, and gender. Eye contact was the behavior mentioned most often as a signal to the user that the librarian was approachable. Talking on the phone was the most frequently mentioned impediment to approachability. The user's decision to initiate an interaction is influenced both by the present impression and by prior experiences with and/or opinions of librarians. Radford notes that nonverbal communication comes bundled in groups of related cues. Because these cues are subtle, quickly exchanged, and complex, Radford recommends videotaping reference interactions for more in-depth analysis of nonverbal behavior. (annotated by Tom Peters)

Saracevic, Tefko, Paul Kantor, Alice Y. Chamis, and Donna Trivison. 1988. A study of information seeking and retrieving. *Journal of the American Society for Information Science* 39: 161–216.

> The authors conducted a series of observations and experiments to learn more about the user's context of questions posed during information retrieval. They also wanted to provide a structure and classification scheme for questions, and study the cognitive traits and decision-making processes of mediated searchers. The study was conducted between 1985 and 1987 to provide scientifically valid, quantified observation on several aspects of the processes whereby humans pose queries to and retrieve information from information systems. Five types of entities were studied as aspects of the information-seeking and retrieval cycle: users, questions, searchers, searches, and items retrieved. Forty users responded to an advertisement and volunteered to participate. Data were collected via questionnaires and audiotaped interviews. Thirty-six paid outside searchers agreed to search the DIALOG databases. Each question was searched only in one database by five of the outside searchers, and by four of the project searchers. The basis for the statistical analysis was user evaluation of retrieval items. The relationships among the variables were analyzed and displayed using the BMDP (originally BioMedical Data Programs) and Statistical Package for the Social Sciences (SPSS) software. A macroanalysis was performed at the search level, followed by a microanalysis at the item level. This is a massive project, worthy of careful study. (revised by Tom Peters)

* Sjolander, Elsa, and Richard Sjolander. 1995. A strategic analysis of the delivery of service in two library reference departments. *College & Research Libraries* 56: 60–70.

> Strategic management can be an effective tool for managing libraries as service organizations. To examine the extent to which libraries have adopted new management practices, the authors used a five-task model to analyze and compare the reference services at the libraries of Florida State University and the University of West Florida in Pensacola. According to the authors, strategic manage-

ment in libraries should compare the philosophy and mission of the reference department, reference policy objectives, the types of clientele served, the reference services provided to meet the objectives, measures of service quality, the availability of reference librarians, the quality and adequacy of the collection, and the evaluation and control of service quality. The authors used several methods to conduct the study: personal interviews with reference department heads, observations, and analyses of policy documents. An open-ended questionnaire was constructed for the interview and a follow-up questionnaire was sent to the department heads. The authors concluded that although the two universities differ in size and type of clientele, they are quite similar from a strategic management perspective. Both libraries have means of measuring service quantity, but neither institution has totally embraced strategic management by objectives and neither institution has any specific measures or standards for the evaluation of service quality in the reference department. (annotated by Razia Nanji)

* Thorne, Rosemary, and Jo Bell Whitlatch. 1994. Patron online catalog success. *College & Research Libraries* 54: 479–497.

Thorne and Whitlatch present how to use a variety of qualitative and quantitative evaluation methods to obtain more detailed information. The purpose of their research was to examine the difference between students using the online catalog with and without assistance. The qualitative research methodology was a combination of surveys and participant observation. This combination allowed librarians to get at more comprehensive and detailed information. The authors also show how to organize and analyze statistical data, which were used to make real changes at their library. Although the study does not focus on reference evaluation, the methodologies and techniques can be adapted in both public and academic libraries. This is a practical, useful, well-organized article, which successfully utilizes qualitative research. (annotated by Elaina Norlin)

* Tillotson, Joy, Joan Cherry, and Marshall Clinton. 1995. Internet use through the University of Toronto Library: Demographics, destinations, and users' reactions. *Information Technology and Libraries* 14: 190–198.

The researchers studied where users went on the Internet when they gained access through UTLink, a DRA (Data Research Associates) Information Gateway online catalog at the University of Toronto. The Hytelnet software (version 6.3) was used to launch the telnet sessions. The number of Internet destinations available through this system at the time of the study was 1,325. Data were collected via an online survey, focus groups, and logs of telnet sessions. The online survey was offered to every fourth user who chose the "Internet Resources" choice on the OPAC menu between December 15, 1993, and January 27, 1994. The two focus groups were conducted by two marketing students, and the sessions were videotaped. Analysis of the logs of the telnet sessions enabled the researchers to identify the most popular destinations, as well as to compare the usage patterns of Internet resources against well-known usage patterns of other types of information systems. The results indicated that 83 percent (1,100) of the 1,325 possible Internet destinations were visited by at least one UTLink user during the study period. Thirteen percent of the available Internet sites accounted for 80 percent of the telnet sessions. The authors recommend that library staff members try to discover the popular sites at their location and become familiar with them. While the findings in this study are out of date, the methodology could still be used today. (annotated by Tom Peters)

* Tygett, Mary, V. Lonnie Lawson, and Kathleen Weessies. 1996. Using undergraduate marketing students in an unobtrusive reference evaluation. *RQ* 36: 270–276.

This unobtrusive survey of reference services was part of a larger assessment of reference services conducted at Central Missouri State University's library. Undergraduate marketing students were chosen to participate (and receive college credit) because of their prior familiarity with subject data collection and evaluation. Each student visited the library twice to engage in two separate reference transactions. After each reference encounter they were asked to complete a fourteen-question survey rating thirteen individual service factors and the overall reference encounter. The survey questions focused on elements of patron perception of service and did not include a measure of accuracy. Students then participated in focus groups in which they discussed their encounters. Finally they submitted written reports of their encounters. Forty of a possible fifty surveys were returned. Responses were grouped by time of day, and this breakdown provided valuable insights and perspectives on the provision of service. Focus group discussions focused on problems found and possible solutions to improving the quality of reference service. The written reports also supplied worthwhile informal information. Statistical analysis of the survey scores did not reveal significant correlations. It was felt, however, that the methodology was sound and that repeating the study for comparison of data could be worthwhile. (annotated by Jeanette Moore Piquet)

Von Seggern, Marilyn. 1989. Evaluating the interview. *RQ* 29: 260–265.

Von Seggern reports on the trial use of the Marilyn D. White method for applying guidelines to the reference interview as a departmental method of evaluation and assessment. Data were collected in April 1988 via audiotaping of reference interviews, comments made by reference librarians as they listened to their taped interviews, the Reference Transaction Assessment Instrument developed by Murfin and Gugelchuk, and observer notes. Five reference librarians participated in audiotaping librarian interviews with patrons. Patrons were informed that audiotaping was in progress, and their permission to be recorded also was recorded. A total of twenty-seven interviews were transcribed using some of the transcription conventions established by Wayne Crouch and Joseph Lucia. The reference librarians themselves met in groups of five to analyze the batches of transcribed interviews. The analysis groups came to the conclusion that recognizing and improving interviewing skills is a continuous process. Von Seggern notes that the method is strong because of its multiple data-gathering channels, but it is too intrusive and time-consuming to be used frequently in a reference assessment program. (revised by Tom Peters)

See also the annotations in the following sections in part IV:

Chapter 1—Quality of Reference Service Resources: Richardson (1998);

Chapter 5: Nardi and O'Day (1996).

CONTRIBUTORS

Laura Dale Bischof is a reference librarian with the MINITEX Library Information Network located at the University of Minnesota. She provides backup reference services to public library systems in Minnesota. From 1998 to 2000 she was a member of the Cooperative Reference Services Committee, Management and Operation of User Services Section (MOUSS), Reference and User Services Association (RUSA) of the American Library Association (ALA). She has also been a long-standing member of the ALA's Western European Subject Specialists Section.

Jacob Carlson is a resident reference librarian and visiting instructor at the University of Illinois at Chicago.

Susan Clark is a reference librarian and bibliographic instruction coordinator at the University of the Pacific in Stockton, California.

Paula Contreras is the assistant documents librarian at the University of Illinois at Chicago.

Frank Elliott is an engineering reference librarian and bibliographer at the Walter Science and Engineering Library at the University of Minnesota, Twin Cities Campus. He is working on his preliminaries for a Ph.D. in sociotechnological planning at the School of Architecture and Urban Planning of the University of Michigan, Ann Arbor. His areas of research expertise are in survey research and program evaluation.

Patricia L. Gregory has been head of reference at Pius XII Library, Saint Louis University, since 1988. In addition to RUSA committee work, she is currently writing a doctoral dissertation in American studies.

A. Craig Hawbaker is head of reference and collection development at the University of the Pacific in Stockton, California. He was co-chair of the RUSA MOUSS Evaluation of Reference and Adult Services Planning Committee which presented "Assessing Current and Future Reference Services" at the 1998 RUSA Institute in Indianapolis.

Lorrie Knight is the electronic services reference librarian at the University of the Pacific in Stockton, California.

John Mess is a librarian in the staff development and training team of the University of Minnesota Libraries. His principal role is as an instructional technologist, developing resources and training for staff in the use of existing and new technologies including office products, multimedia development, and Internet technologies.

Razia Nanji is a humanities and social-sciences services reference librarian and a selector in the reference collection management team at the George A. Smathers Libraries of the University of Florida. She is also the coordinator for the e-mail reference services for the libraries.

Elaina Norlin works as an undergraduate services librarian at the University of Arizona. In addition to regular reference and bibliographic instruction duties, Elaina has designed, coordinated, and implemented a four-step qualitative reference evaluation for the main and science reference desks. She became interested in qualitative research while working with advertising and marketing faculty members during her undergraduate studies. Elaina has an M.L.I.S. degree and a B.A. in advertising.

Eric Novotny is currently assistant reference librarian at the University of Illinois at Chicago. He has served on the RUSA MOUSS Evaluation of Reference and Adult Services Committee since 1995.

Mary Parker is assistant director and electronic resources officer of the MINITEX Library Information Network located at the University of Minnesota. She coordinates a backup reference referral program for public library systems in Minnesota. She was the chair of the RUSA MOUSS Evaluation of Reference and Adult Services Committee for 1997–99.

Thomas A. Peters is the dean of university libraries at Western Illinois University in Macomb. He is serving as guest editor of an upcoming *Library Trends* theme issue on assessing digital library services. His most recent book is *Computerized Monitoring and Online Privacy* (McFarland, 1999).

Jeanette Moore Piquet is a regional branch manager with the St. Louis Public Library. She received her undergraduate degree in art history from the State University of New York at Geneseo and her M.L.S. from the University of Missouri at Columbia.

Jim Stemper is coordinator of reference services for remote users at the University of Minnesota Libraries, Twin Cities Campus. The position is part of a grant-funded project to provide library support for distance learning.

Jo Bell Whitlatch is reference librarian and a history and political science selector at San Jose State University Library. She also teaches occasionally in the Graduate School of Library and Information Science at San Jose. She was president of the Reference and User Services and Association (RUSA) of the American Library Association for 1998–99. She has published several articles and books on reference evaluation.

INDEX